THE Wines
AND LANDSCAPES
OF SPAIN

THE Wines
AND LANDSCAPES
OF SPAIN

JEREMY WATSON

Illustrations by
MURRAY ZANONI

PAVILION

First published in Great Britain in 2000 by
Pavilion Books Limited
London House, Great Eastern Wharf, Parkgate Road,
London SW11 4NQ

Text © Jeremy Watson 2000
Illustrations © Murray Zanoni 2000
The moral right of the author has been asserted.

Designed by Janet James

A CIP catalogue record for this book is available from the British Library.

ISBN 1 86205 400 2

Colour reproduction by Colour AGP (Repro) Ltd, Hong Kong
Printed and bound in Spain by Graficas Reunidas

1 3 5 7 9 10 8 6 4 2

This book may be ordered by post direct from the publisher.
Please contact the marketing department. But try your bookshop first.

Contents

INTRODUCTION

The transformation of the image and quality of Spanish wines during the last quarter of the twentieth century has been nothing less than remarkable. Having said that, it is not such a surprise to some connoisseurs, who believed it was only a matter of time, and know that there are still many more exciting changes to come.

As someone who has been working with Spanish wines for more than thirty years, I have witnessed the changes firsthand. It is no coincidence that the metamorphosis followed more than forty years of isolation, despite the tourism industry, during General Franco's dictatorship. Following his death in 1975, the phlegmatic character of the nation allowed a relatively smooth and swift conversion to democratic government, the influences of which filtered quickly into the infrastructure of business.

A few pioneers were already introducing new wine technology, but were inhibited by a lack of interest in their new, fruitier styles of wines. It was a classic catch-22 situation. The solution was found through the combined efforts of those winemaking pioneers, some very committed distributors, and imaginative and appealing advertising and promotion. This is where Murray Zanoni came in. His delightfully sympathetic and emotive water-colours were exactly what was needed to introduce the outside world to the real and forgotten Spain.

Through imaginative use of Murray's work, Wines from Spain (the United Kingdom office of the Instituto Español de Comercio Exterior in Madrid) was able to drip-feed the message to a suspicious public and trade. It is hard now to recall the bigoted attitude towards Spanish wines prevalent at that time. But it was my good fortune to oversee this campaign, and to work closely with Murray as we witnessed a steady conversion of opinion.

The campaign started in the United Kingdom because it has long been the shop window of the wine world, and what happens there is invariably reflected in other countries later. In 1997, and as a direct result of the campaign Murray and I were invited to do work for the Vinopolis wine experience project in London. You will find a number of the paintings he produced for the Iberian room reproduced in this book.

The book is an informal and relaxed look at the subject, and there is not always a sequence to the text and pictures. I have written about the regions and aspects that I believe are the most interesting, and have kept technical terms to a minimum, explaining the few I use, hopefully satisfactorily.

The names of regions and cities are given in Spanish: in other words I have avoided Anglicized names such as Seville (instead of Sevilla), or Catalonia (instead of Cataluña). I do not believe personal and place names should be changed between Latin languages.

Since the list of people whose assistance we would like to thank most sincerely for their kindnesses would read like a catalogue of the Spanish wine industry, I propose to name only Miguel Torres, Carlos Falco, the Marqués de Griñon and Francisco Valencia for their endorsements, and Colin Webb at Pavilion Books for his support and the confidence he has shown in us.

Background

      A little history. Bread is considered a key gauge of economic and social history. While I cannot pretend that wine could ever hold the same siginificance, it is a fact that wherever conquerors went the vine was an essential part of their baggage.

As far as we can tell, the wine vine (vitis vinifera) originated in Iran, but came to Spain from Egypt with the Phoenicians. They landed in Spain in around 2000 BC, first at Málaga, then at Cádiz, homes to two of the greatest fortified wines – Málaga and Sherry.

The Romans followed, arriving at Tarragona in 200 BC, and introduced the vine as they marched north in Cataluña, and west along the River Ebro to Aragón, Navarra, Rioja and Castilla-León. The Vandals and Visigoths were not too concerned with the juice of the grape, but the Moors, who arrived in AD 711, proved to be an exception despite what one might think today.

The Moors loved the sweet non-alcoholic grape juice resulting from the high sugar content of the fruit, so cultivation of the vine continued and a blind eye was turned to the making of wine. Originally the Koran did not forbid the consumption of wine, but it later included diktats that threatened dire consequences for anyone who should become inebriated, so clearly a policy of abstinence is considered safer.

The final departure of the Moors in 1492 heralded the arrival of the Golden Age of Spain and one of the great Empires. Christopher Columbus sailed for the 'Indies', only to discover the Americas. Thus began the age of the conquering Conquistadors, who (as usual) took the vine with them, planting it in California, Central and South America, and bringing back other untold riches that the State managed to squander through extravagance and bad housekeeping.

Meanwhile, agriculture was stagnating in Spain, because landowners were interested only in hunting and shooting, and boasting the expanses of their enormous estates. It was invaders of the peaceful sort who kick-started things when, in the late eighteenth century, British and Irish wine merchants arrived in Jerez to develop the Sherry industry with which we are familiar today. Next came the French from Bordeaux who, following the devastation of their vineyards by Phylloxera at the end of the nineteenth century, crossed the Pyrenees to Rioja, and introduced better vineyard practices and improved oak-barrel ageing techniques. Finally came the winemakers of the late twentieth century – French and British again, plus Australians, New Zealanders, Californians and Chileans – while Spanish winemakers took their skills to the Americas and China.

PRIDE AND PASSION

The Spanish nation is often (and mistakenly in my opinion) described as Latin, though their love of life certainly betrays elements of that culture. However, such a term is too simplistic. The Spanish are a very proud yet phlegmatic people, in some ways reserved but uninhibited, both patient and courteous, although apparently sometimes intolerant and inconsiderate. Their willingness to learn has been important in the transformation of winemaking.

They are passionate about many things, not least the family and football, and generous to a fault in both manner and hospitality (*mi casa es su casa* – my house is your house). Spaniards will go to great lengths to assist someone they have never met before; they will insist you pass through a door first, but they are unlikely to give way to you in traffic. Certainly Spaniards are more punctual these days, but they retain a healthy disregard for time.

TRAVELLING

Before 1975, few Spaniards travelled within Spain, let alone abroad, and the pattern of life rotated around the provincial capitals, both bureaucratically and for the distribution of goods. So, the huge improvements in communications by road, rail and air have brought a greater awareness of what is beyond those old boundaries, to every aspect of life, including the wine revolution.

THE PARADORS

These are the state-owned hotels, which were conceived by King Alfonso XIII, and have been an important stimulus to tourism in the interior. The first was opened in 1926 in the Sierra de Gredos, west of Madrid and chosen for its spectacular views. The group now boasts more than eighty-five hotels built in restored convents, castles and palaces, many with magnificent views, and often sited in remote locations. They offer stylish accommodation, specialize in the regional gastronomy and function as shop windows for an area's wines.

13

GEOGRAPHY AND WEATHER

The environmental and climatic conditions in Spain are among the best for growing vines, and it was only the insularity of the country and backward nature of the industry that prevented the country's winemakers from being more successful, sooner.

The country occupies some 80 per cent of the Iberian Peninsular on the south-western tip of Europe, to which it is connected by the boundary with France. Thus the peninsular is almost an island, which experiences several starkly contrasting climatic influences. These are the prevailing cold and wet Atlantic airflows; the hot Saharan winds from Africa; the warm and gentler Mediterranean; and the cold northerlies descending over the Pyrenees.

Spain is very mountainous, with most of the country lying at an average of over 600 metres (about 2,000 feet) above sea level. The centre consists of a vast plateau, divided into north and south by the mountains of Madrid, and this is known as the *Meseta*. There are other, smaller plateaux in Aragón, Murcia and Extremadura, but the existence of all of them is key to the healthy conditions in which the vines are grown.

The north-west coast is known as Green Spain, and stretches from Galicia through Asturias and Cantabria to the Pyrenees. Here rainfall is high, winters are harsh and summers short. By contrast the Levante, in the opposite corner, has the most ambient climate of the western Mediterranean, and is very dry with well over 3,000 hours of sunshine annually.

The technical term for the climate of the centre is Continental, which, again, is dry and sunny, but the temperatures are often subzero in winter for days on end. Together with the varying mixes of chalky clay soils, it is this that makes Spanish vineyards and their fruit so healthy, with high sugar levels ensuring good alcoholic content, a fundamental requirement for producing quality wines.

WINE RIVERS

Water is a vital resource for growing vines, even though they have roots that search deep down for the water table. Most of the world's great wine regions are in river valleys, and experience the many macro- and microclimatic conditions they and the surrounding terrain create.

The Iberian Peninsular boasts several substantial watercourses, all but one flowing into the Atlantic. The exception is the largest of all – the Ebro, which rises in the mountains above Santander on the north coast, and exits into the Mediterranean at Amposta in the south of Tarragona province. It is best known for its influence on Rioja.

The Duero flows west through Castilla-León before becoming the Douro and exiting at Oporto in Portugal. The Tajo rises east of Madrid and also changes its name to become the Tagus that exits at Lisbon. The other important rivers are the Guadiana and the Guadalquivir in the south, and the Miño and Sil in Galicia.

Spanish Wines –
The Quiet Revolution*

The Spanish have been quick to learn the new technology and how to use it. The arrival of young Spanish winemakers alongside visiting winemakers, is carrying the revolution forward at a pace that belies their inexperience.

Spain has the largest area of land under vine, yet is only the third-largest producer of wine, thanks to low rainfall. Until recently almost all vines were bush varieties, or pruned as such, to make them grow low to the ground so as to garner every drop of moisture, but modern vine-yard technology is taking over with vines trained on posts and wires.

Spain produces all types of wines – red, white, pink, sparkling, fortified, dry, sweet, young, old, oak-aged, traditional and new wave. The revolution started in the Bodegas, with the introduction of stainless steel vats in place of concrete ones, and temperature-control equipment to slow fermentation. The improvement was immediate, the old 'hot' wines produced by tumultuous, high-temperature fermentation disappeared, to be replaced by fresh and fruity ones.

* This is also the title of a video made for the Instituto Español de Comercio Exterior by Robert Joseph in 1997, in which I was heavily involved.

The 'new' process prevents the fruit drying out, and the wines began to show a vivacity and brilliance that had been sorely missing. At this point, the producers were prompted to go back to the beginning, realizing the benefit that better raw materials would add.

They tested the soils and their suitability to the different vine varieties; they chose better clones of some varieties; introduced training on posts and wires (*espaldera*) with drip irrigation in the drier zones; improved pruning techniques; created better canopies; and selected the fruit more carefully.

The investment of money and time is paying off – so much so that the demand in some areas is exceeding supply. Nobody would have conceived such a phenomenon in Spain twenty years ago.

IRRIGATION

This is one of the secrets behind the winemaking revolution. Historically, it meant drowning the vineyards in excess quantities of water, which inflated production and ruined the quality of the fruit, so it was rightly banned. The severe drought of 1991 to 1995 led to a rethink and change of attitude towards the process because ten per cent of the vines were dying.

The more sophisticated drip irrigation system was and is being widely used elsewhere, being designed to improve the quality of the grapes, rather than increase the volume of production. The system ensures a balanced, slow supply of water to the vines in those regions where dry, hot conditions prevail. But the investment is only worthwhile if the vines are trained on posts and wires so as to allow the bunches of grapes to get sufficient sunlight and ripen evenly. Without drip irrigation the grapes of the vines trained on wires would shrivel in the heat.

VINE VARIETIES

Many of the vine varieties planted in Spain were chosen because they could survive in intense heat, with little water, yet be reasonably prolific. The result is too many rather dull varieties that find little favour outside Spain. Fortunately there are others that can sit alongside

the best in the world. New vineyard technology has revived interest in many indigenous vines and encouraged the planting of others that could not be considered until now, and these include ubiquitous foreign ones such as Cabernet Sauvignon, Merlot and Chardonnay.

Some experts debate the ethics of Spain introducing foreign vine

varieties, though why Spain should be denied the inclusion of the outsiders, when the rest of the world is using them, is a mystery to me. The red varieties have been particularly successful, and have been a huge stimulus to better winemaking, if only because Spanish winemakers can compare their results with those in other countries.

They have found that, apart from improving the wines from their own varieties, foreign varieties allow an extra dimension to their wines.

Another important aspect is that the Bodegas are increasing the area of vineyards under their ownership, or that they contract with independent farmers. This way they control as much of the fruit as possible, which is a sure way of having the chance to make better wines. (The best of the red and white varietals all reappear individually in other parts of this book, and a list can be found in the Appendix.)

A BODEGA

This is the name given to a Winery in Spain. Originally the buildings were designed to be cool, with high, thick, walls, small, high windows and painted white to reflect the sun. The basic design is similar today, but more and more are introducing ventilation systems to ensure a regular temperature is maintained, winter and summer.

WINE LAW

In Europe producers are governed by legislation of the European Union, national governments, regional authorities and local controlling councils. Fundamentally, and briefly, wine-producing regions in Europe are classified into two categories:

1. Quality wine – q.w.p.s.r. (*Vino de Calidad – v.c.p.r.d.*) is a Denomination of Origin (DO) or a Denomination of Origin Calificada (DOCa).
2. Table Wine (*Vino de Mesa*) including *Vinos de La Tierra* (*Vins du Pays* in France) and *Vinos Comarcales*.

A Denomination of Origin (DO) – category 1 above – is a Quality Wine produced in a Demarcated Region. It is controlled by a Regulating Council, known as the *Consejo Regulador de la Denominación de Origen*, followed by the name of the relevant wine region. The Council has control of the origin of the grapes, production

regulations and quality control, but often has to bow to higher authorities with regard to packaging and labelling. Any wine originating in a DO will have the words *Denominación de Origen* with the name of the region on the label.

Calificada (DOCa) is the description for a higher status awarded to wine regions that have established a reputation for making very good quality wines over a long period. Rioja is the only region in Spain to be so classified thus far. *Calificada*, in this usage, means 'Superior'. Certain measuring criteria are applied so that it is not just a matter of opinion.

Vinos de la Tierra are a select category of *Vinos de Mesa* that have not been much in evidence, because of the push to establish more Denominations of Origin and benefit from EU subsidies. The regulations governing Vinos de la Tierra and Vinos Comarcales allow some flexibility and a number of producers have realised the benefits, preferring to forgo subsidies and work without the higher status of DO. The success of highly rated estates such as Abadía Retuerta, Dehesa del Carrizal, Dominio de Valdepusa, Manzaneque, Mauro, Otero, Alta Pavina, Pers and Valonga, have proved that, in the right hands, such a decision is justified.

BACK LABELS

Spain makes extensive use of back labels and precintas (smaller slip labels either on the back or over the cork). They are both officially required by all Regulating Councils of the DOs for control purposes, and used as a marketing tool to provide more information about the wines and the producers.

Some of the official ones, like those in Rioja contain useful information – vintage and ageing period in particular, while others are less helpful to the consumer except to confirm the bottle's provenance.

Winemaking and Wines

Winemaking is a term foreign to leading European wine-producing countries, and there is no translation into their languages. It comes from the New World, and describes the total activity and responsibility for the production of a wine, from the vineyard to the bottle.

In Europe, the process was divided into three by the traditional structure of wine production. Vineyards belonged to farmers, who sold grapes to those who fermented the musts into wines, and who, in turn, sold them to Bodegas for ageing, bottling and commercialization. The system still exists, in part, and is represented by the Co-operatives that function in every agricultural town and village where vines are grown.

OAK BARRELS

The Englishman in me says barrels are for beer, and casks are for wine, or even whisky if they have had Sherry in them. But the Spanish for cask is *barrica*, which sounds more like barrel, and other, more cognizant experts suggest this word is more widely used. So barrel it is.

Oak barrels of 225 litres have become the standard for maturing wines in Spain, but ageing a wine in oak means very little unless we are told more about the origin of the oak, and the type and age of the barrels. There is nothing wrong in ageing wines in old, clean oak barrels, but it is an expensive way of doing things, since the wood will be little more than a storage container, and the same results can be achieved in a vat. New oak, or nearly new oak, is most suited to modern winemaking, but sometimes both new and old are used for the same wine, with the components being blended together at a later stage.

Most oak used in Spain is American (chiefly Virginian), but French oak (from Nevers and Allier) is also popular. French is twice the price of American oak because more wood is needed to make the barrel, since the wood is split rather than cut, meaning only 20 per cent of the tree can be used. In keeping with their nationalities, the vanillin aromas and flavours are rich and powerful in American oak, while they are more subtle and release more slowly in the French.

Oak is costly, the most expensive barrels being around 75,000 pesetas ($500 or 450 Euros), and supply is a problem, so more oak is being sought in places like Bosnia and Russia. Whichever the origin, an oak barrel has an effective life of no more than ten years before the flavours disappear. So a Bodega is replacing around 10 per cent of its stock every year.

WINE

Contrary to general belief, wine is not a living thing. Whoever heard of two bottles making love and producing a miniature? But it does contain living bodies. Wine is made by fermenting the juices of almost any fruit, but, in the context of this book, it is the alcoholic drink produced by the fermentation of the juice of fresh grapes. Particular to wines in Spain are the thousands of hours of sunshine that encourage high sugar content in the grapes and give good alcohol levels, resulting in wines that are more stable than those with lower alcohol levels. After that, it is down to the skills of those who make the wines.

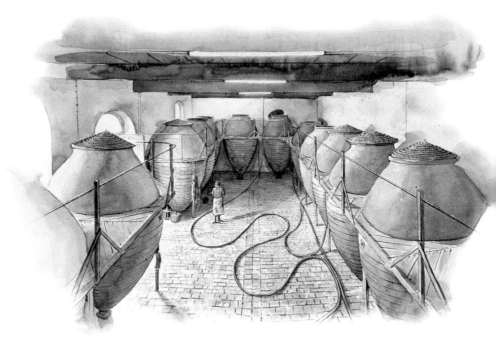

WHITES

Not so long ago I went into a bar in Córdoba and asked for a dry white wine. The waiter brought a Jerez Fino, not a bad idea, but not what I wanted or asked for, so he tried again with a Montilla Fino which he described as half dry, wrong again. Finally, he understood what I meant and exclaimed 'Ah! Blanco dulce!', whereupon he brought a bottle of Valdepeñas dry white. This is not to put down the waiter, but to demonstrate that there were curious ideas in Spain of what was, or is, white wine, and there is still a lower level of interest in them today; curious in such a warm climate.

Spain makes top-quality white wines with both indigenous and imported grape varieties, but it is proving a hard message to get across. So little white wine is consumed, indeed more pink is drunk, that consumers do not have the white habit as they do for red. Now winemakers have discovered more about the better properties of the grape varieties and have started producing white wines that far outstrip their predecessors. We can only hope that Spaniards will discover the liquid gold in their midst, because, at all price levels, there are wines to compete with many better-established ones from other countries.

We consumers must take some of the blame for the ubiquity and sameness of white wines, preferring to save our extravagance for the reds. But, to get equal enjoyment from a white wine as we do from a red we need to pay more for the white. Imperfections in white wines can be masked by the subtle use of a little sugar, but that destroys the dryness of the wine, while with reds, the little shortcomings are masked by the robustness of the wine. The solution is in our hands.

PINKS

Don't be swayed by the shopkeeper or waiter, who will try to offload his older pink wines by telling you older is better, even though some of them really believe it.

It is essential that pink wines are drunk young – the younger the better, when they have that all-important brightness and freshness. Such a pink wine is a pleasure to drink, and not only on a summer's day. Unfortunately, too many of us have experienced beery-tasting old pinks, the colour of old onions, that can prejudice us against them for life. In Spain, pinks are big business and stock rotation is fast, but in other countries, where sales are slow, bottles grow old on the shelves.

Pink wines are called *rosados* in Spain. They are, in fact, very light red wines made from the first, free-run juice of red grapes that have macerated with their skins for just a few hours (remember, the flesh of a black grape is white, it is the skins that give the colour). So, though often sold at the same price as young white wines, *rosados* are more expensive to make.

Myths have built up around pink wines to suggest they are only suitable in warm weather, but why should that be if we are happy to drink cold white wines in summer and winter? Then there are those who are convinced that pink wine is not serious and something of a compromise, but neither is true. These are wines in a category of their own, being a colourful and lively aperitif, or wines that go well with fish dishes, white meats (turkey at Christmas?), and are well suited to pasta, rice and vegetarian food.

REDS

These are predominant in Spain, firstly because of the cold climate of the interior, where throughout much of the year, low temperatures encourage a robust *cocina* (food culture). Rioja has been the dominant red wine for a long time, even though good reds were and are produced in other regions. Rioja has always been considered the most classical and correct, while wines of other regions were thought to be strictly for the local bars.

Change is on the way: the world-wide popularity of Rioja has put pressure on supply and prices, and is forcing people to look elsewhere. As a result people are discovering wines made on their own doorsteps that surpass their expectations, and in several instances wines that have often been developed by foreign winemakers.

Spaniards love oak, as to a lesser extent do many others (the British in particular), so oak is becoming a greater element in the making of red wines. Of course, young wines are still the basic diet but it is the demand from abroad that has driven the development of the new wave of young fruity reds.

SPARKLING

In recent years the Cava sparkling wines have established themselves on a world-wide basis as attractive, easy to drink and good value. A chapter is given over to them later on.

FORTIFIED

Spain produces several fortified wines – Sherry, Málaga, Montilla and the Moscatels, among them. When wines are fortified, the producers add alcohol distilled from white wine and nothing else. All four regions are covered in separate sections in the book.

AGUJA

A slightly sparkling or petillant wine made mostly in Cataluña, Aguja is quite often semi-sweet and very popular with young people, but quite pricey for what it is.

SANGRIA

This is not a wine in the pure sense, but wine-based. It is also immensely popular and widely consumed. Everyone has their own recipe, and some are pretty mind-boggling, but real Sangria is a simple, delightfully refreshing drink made in a large jug with a full-bodied red wine, twice the amount of fizzy lemonade and a dash of brandy, garnished with slices of orange and lemon, and lots of ice. If you prefer it dry, use fizzy water.

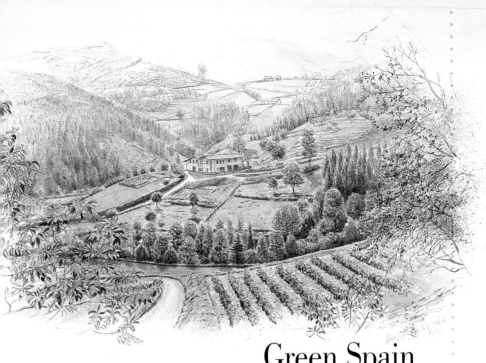

Green Spain

Along the north coast of the country from Galicia to the Pyrenees lies Green Spain, owing its name to the fact that the Atlantic winds bring regular rainfall and warm, yet short summers, resulting in fertile, verdant hillsides and pastures. It is made up of the four autonomous regions of Galicia, Asturias, Cantabria and the Pàis Vasco all sandwiched between the Sierra Cantabria and the Bay of Biscay.

GALICIA

Gallegos, in the past, drank some pretty awful stuff, both from the region, and shipped in from elsewhere in Spain. Then, in the 1980s, they discovered the real value of the jewel in their midst, the Albariño grape which was given a different dimension by new technology.

Galicia is a unique territory and often compared to parts of Northern Europe. It is green and fertile, where most things are on a smaller scale than elsewhere in Spain. The steep, hilly terrain, the narrow, tortuous roads, the farms (some of which are still medieval), and the heavier concentration of population are all reminiscent of a country like Britain. The climate is wet and the language has similarities with Portuguese. Galicia's main economic activity stems from the Spanish fishing fleet, much of which is based at the ports of Vigo and La Coruña.

RIAS BAIXAS

These are the low fiords of the Galician coast, around Pontevedra. The higher and more severe Rias Altas are to the north, around La Coruña. The wine region of the Rias Baixas is made up of small vineyards, where the vines are often trained more than a metre off the ground on *pergolas* – special frames designed to keep the grapes clear of the wet ground, and allow maximum exposure to the sun. The viticulture is intensive and time consuming, the Bodegas are economical to run, but the small scale of production and erratic vintages lead to high costs.

Rias Baixas is divided into three zones: Val do Sanés near Pontevedra city, Condado de Tea on the river Miño at Tea, and O Rosal further downstream towards A Garda on the coast. Some Bodegas blend in other local varieties, but it is the Albariño that puts Rias Baixas at the top of the tree for Spanish white wines.

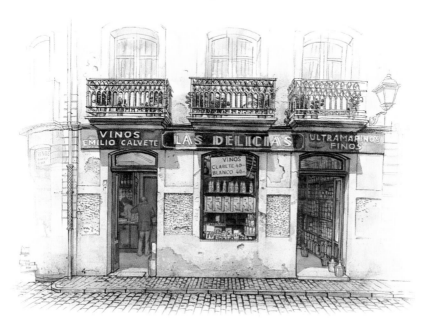

ALBARIÑO

This is the vine of Rias Baixas. Though it is a little pricey, it produces one of Spain's best white wines – aromatic with a delicate combination of apples and fennel, good acidity and length. Some people think that it is related to the Rhine Riesling, while others have detected similarities with Viognier from the Rhône, which is enough to make one think it is probably unique.

It is well worth visiting one of the many seafood restaurants of the region, like El Tunel in Baiona, and indulging in a glorious array of shellfish and a bottle of Albariño – the epitome of hedonism.

THE PILGRIMS' ROUTE OF ST JAMES
EL CAMINO DE SANTIAGO

This is probably the world's first Wine Route. Pilgrims trek along roads and paths from the Pyrenees, across the north of Spain to the shrine of Saint James (*San Jacabo*) in the Cathedral at Santiago de Compostella. Mainly travelling on foot, but a few on bicycles or even on horseback, they make the journey which, depending on fitness and feet, distractions and detours, takes some forty to fifty days. It brings them through lovely countryside and the wine regions in Navarra, Rioja, Burgos, León, Bierzo, Valdeorras and Lugo.

GODELLO

An early ripening, white grape variety recommended in the other four wine regions of Galicia, not least Valdeorras where La Tapada makes the outstanding Guitian. Its delightfully delicate flavours of green apples with floral aromas have brought it to prominence both here and in Bierzo in León. It is another example of how the new technology has shown winemakers unexpected treasure in their midst. I put it in the top three of the indigenous white varieties, with Albariño and Verdejo.

AGUARDIENTE

The Gallegos distil a dry spirit called Aguardiente from almost any vegetative product available. But, the *crème de la crème* is Orujo, which is distilled from the pips, skins and lees of the pressed grapes.

It is a popular postprandial all over Spain but nowhere as highly prized as it is in Galicia.

ASTURIAS

The Principality of Spain, of which the son of King Juan Carlos and Queen Sofia holds the title, Principe Felipe of Asturias. Historically the region thrived on coal-mining, steel refineries and shipbuilding around Gijon and Oviedo, but, as elsewhere, these are in decline. Very little wine is produced, but there is a strong tradition of drinking good-quality wines, from Rioja in particular.

FABADA

A speciality of Asturias, *fabada* is a white bean stew made with belly of pork, gammon and sausage (*chorizo*). It is particularly suited to a cold day when washed down with a good wine, but beware, half a portion is invariably more than enough for all but the stoutest eaters.

THE PICOS EUROPA

A particularly stunning and dramatic section of the Northern Sierra lying on the border of Asturias and Cantabria provinces. Amid this scenery of sheer-sided gorges and vertical rock faces, the goat's milk produces an outstanding, soft-textured blue cheese, called Cabrales.

CANTABRIA

Much of this lovely province is like a mini-Switzerland, with expensive, rolling green pastures. As in Asturias, the people consume the better-quality wines from other regions, and a friend in Barcelona has convinced me that Santander, the capital, has the best wine bars in Spain.

There is a small wine area around Potes on the edge of the Picos Europa. Thanks to the persistence of a few families wanting to fill their cellars, interest has been maintained in the vine through a period when the people might well have given up on them. They make a light red that they call *tostadilla* from Mencìa red and Palomino white grapes; but with new technology, who knows, the business could well become more commercial.

THE BASQUE COUNTRY

This region is as lovely as Cantabria, yet individual in appearance. As soon as one moves a short distance inland the terrain rises to 600 or 700 metres (2,000 feet), creating a narrow coastal strip, which emphasises the minimalism one associates with Galicia. The Swiss-chalet-style rooftops of the small farms tucked away in undulating countryside, and the villages with tortuous Basque names contrast with the heavy yet declining industrial environment of Bilbao. It is exciting to see how the city is being stylishly redeveloped, and how popular a destination the advent of the Guggenheim Museum has made it.

There are few places in Spain where one can expect to eat better, especially the seafood.

MODERN SPAIN

Modern Spain was one of the requirements in the brief given to us by Vinopolis. Without the inspired decision of the City fathers of Bilbao to build the extraordinarily innovative Frank Geary design of the Guggenheim museum, this would have been tough, because most modern city skylines look identical, and nothing else we saw was particularly inspiring.

Imagine my concern, then, when Murray said the Guggenheim would not work as a water-colour. He was worried by the titanium grey which, combined with the building's shape, he felt deprived him of the opportunity to project it effectively on to paper. He had demonstrated how some subjects make great photos yet poor paintings, but I was determined we should try. He will admit that I badgered him for weeks, and after three visits, and by chance capturing the golden effect of the early morning sun on the north side, he produced a lovely and original picture. The museum says so much about the determination of all Spaniards to re-establish their country's former greatness.

TXACOLI

A delicate, white wine produced along the coast between the port of Bilbao and San Sebastian, the elite summer resort of Madrileños. Pronounced Chacoli, it is made in two small areas of about eighty

THE WINES AND LANDSCAPES OF SPAIN

hectares each. One near the infamous Guernica in Vizcaya and called, in the vernacular, Bizcaiko-Tzakolina. The other is more sheltered and further east, called Getariako-Txacolina, but a third is emerging in neighbouring Alava. The grape variety is less of a tongue twister, namely Hondarrabi.

THE PORRON

This is a double-spouted drinking vessel for those who do not mind ruining their shirts. Never having mastered it after consigning several items of clothes to the bin, I have unerring admiration for those who can pour a litre of red wine on to their forehead, down the ridge of their nose and into their mouth non-stop.

Castilla-León

There is an extraordinary sense of being transported back in time when crossing the vast, almost deserted wheatlands and sugarbeet fields of Castilla-León. This is the home of the Castillian language, it is 'Classical Spain' with magnificent and historical cities like León, Avila, Salamanca, Segovia and Burgos evoking feelings of awe and splendour. Yet, there is a glorious tranquillity all around.

It was the Kings of León and Asturias who started to push the Moors back to the south, and it was across the nothern plain of Castilla that they fought, a fact reinforced by the line of fortresses along the Duero river valley. They were followed by Isabella of Castilla, who joined with Fernando I of Aragón to begin the unification of Spain. Later the Bourbons adopted Segovia as their summer retreat, with a small, Versailles-like Palace at La Granja, nearby. Everywhere you go the mantle of these events seems to go too, and intensifies the great sense of history.

BIERZO

This wine region on the León border with Galicia is in a closed environment surrounded by mountains and bisected by the River Sil. There is a sense of strong self-sufficiency, probably imbued by the sturdy nature of the slate quarrymen and coal-miners in the mountains, along with the valley farmers.

Godello and Mencía are the preferred indigenous varietals, and early results are very encouraging, as the region strives to rid itself of an image of sending cheap, red wines to the thirsty Gallegos and hard-working Asturians. Part of the programme is to move the vines from the Sil valley, and plant them higher on the south-facing ridge of the Sierra Cantabria, where the fruit will develop better.

MENCIA

A red vine suited to the colder, wetter north-west. Thought to be related to the Cabernet Franc, it yields richly coloured, warm, soft, plummy wines with good length. It probably needs the help of a more tannic variety to make better aged wines.

Vinos de Mesa

These are produced by two well-known wine producers in northern León. Palacio de Arganza makes wines with great age, very much aimed at those who like traditional, old oxidized reds. The other is a company called VILE, unfortunately using one of those acronyms that don't translate well (in Spanish, it is pronounced veelay). Short for Vinos León, it is a large company producing first-rate table wines in the north of the province and employing the Prieto Picudo, a vine variety almost exclusive to this area.

Rancio Wines

These have been made in many parts of Spain, not least in the northern areas. They are Sherry style, sometimes fortified wines made from Palomino grapes, but very poor imitations of the real thing. They were popular with agricultural workers on the *Meseta* during the long hard winters, and with miners, shipbuilders and quarrymen of the harsh north coast.

TORO

Near the Portuguese border Toro is a small and emerging wine region in Zamora. Manuel Fariña pioneered modern winemaking here, bringing attention to the region by making splendid wines and selling them under the brand Colegiata – the name of the town church that overlooks the Roman bridge on the River Duero. Other producers are now catching up and important companies from nearby Rueda and Ribera del Duero are moving in, among them Vega Sicilia, Valduero and Antonio Sanz. The red grape variety is Tinto de Toro, which is related to Tempranillo; and the white is Malvasía.

RUEDA

Some of Spain's best white wines are produced here. Despite the large extent of this mostly flat region, the majority of the 6,000 hectares of vineyards are concentrated on low rolling hills near the southern bank of the River Duero, between Tordesillas and La Seca. Verdejo is a variety almost exclusive to the zone, while Sauvignon Blanc and Viura have been introduced as the Palomino is removed.

Rueda only produces white wines with DO, but several Bodegas produce red wines from Tempranillo under the *Vino de la Tierra* Medina del Campo, and very successfully. The town of Rueda is scattered with shops selling wines, cheeses and oils to visitors from as far as Madrid, who come to restock their cellars and larders.

The producers Marqués de Riscal brought attention to Rueda as long ago as 1970, when they decided to make white wine here rather than in Rioja, and with Antonio Sanz of Bodegas Crianza Castilla la Vieja, among others, they have had a major influence on the new style of wines.

Verdejo

The premier grape variety of Rueda, and one of the three best white varieties in Spain. It is difficult to propagate (which is probably why it does not appear in other regions), but it delivers full round flavours of ripe apples and melon, with floral aromas. Again, new technology has played a major part in bringing the variety to the fore.

SAUVIGNON BLANC

This grape variety has found a foothold in Rueda and Cataluña, being introduced in order to add a popular and 'commercial' style to the wines. It is recognized by its acidic, gooseberry characteristics, but purists do not find the Spanish wines from this variety typical enough. Though it may appear more extensively in Extremadura (see p.101) in the future, it is so widely available in other parts of the world it will probably not assume very great importance in Spain.

RIBERA DEL DUERO

During the last decade of the twentieth century Ribera del Duero became a fashionable variety. But as recently as the 1960s they were replacing vines in the Duero valley with other, more profitable crops, despite the fact that Vega Sicilia at Valbuena de Duero was making the top Spanish wine. Then, in 1982 when the zone was awarded Denomination status, an agricultural engineer called Alejandro Fernández created his Pesquera wine that found such favour with Robert Parker in the USA.

The DO is much smaller than Rioja, and it is a bit like comparing Burgundy with Bordeaux in more senses than one, with the former representing Ribera del Duero. Tinto Fino is the local name for Tempranillo and the dominant variety. The wines must contain a minimum of 75 per cent of this variety when blended with any of Cabernet Sauvignon, Merlot or Garnacha (Grenache in France).

The Duero valley is a difficult environment in which to grow vines, not least because of the early frosts that decimate up to half the vintages, but also because of the dry conditions and short ripening season. Thus production is erratic, which means grape prices are a minefield as they soar to levels that some producers, already strapped for cash, find increasingly difficult to meet. Saddest of all, however, is that too much of the wine is sold too young, and the wines deserve better than that.

TINTO FINO

The Duero name for Tempranillo, and well suited to a region where the ripening season is not much more than the minimum of 100 days. This early-ripening variety (frosts and other climatic conditions permitting), is always ready to deliver good fruit. The same cannot always be said of the Cabernet Sauvignon, which needs longer, and occasionally does not manage to ripen enough.

VEGA SICILIA

Sited on the south bank of the river at Valbuena de Duero, for years Vega Sicilia produced Spain's best and most expensive wine. A *vega* is an alluvial valley and Sicilia is the name of an old chapel in the vineyards. The original owners imported Cabernet Sauvignon during the mid-nineteenth century, and later, brought Merlot and Malbec, all of which they blend with Tinto Fino.

There are three wines. Firstly Unico, which is made in the very best years and never released until it is at least ten years old, and then not

always in order of vintages. Secondly there is Valbuena, which is made every year, barring total disaster, and is released at five years of age. The winemaker at Vega Sicilia recommends the Valbuena in the years when Unico is not made, because all the best fruit is in this wine. Finally, they occasionally make a wine called Reserva Especial, which might be called the Unico of the Unicos.

A few years ago the proprietors invested in a new and totally separate Bodega, calling it Alión, thinking to sell wines that are a bit less exclusive. They have another resounding success on their hands.

CORDERO ASADO

The *cordero asado* of Castilla-León is the most gorgeous roast lamb. Many regions claim lamb as a speciality, but I challenge any to better that of the flocks that graze on the rosemary-carpeted slopes of the Cordiller Iberica, in Burgos and Soria. Served quite differently to the precious little pink medallions of a five-star restaurant, it tumbles off the bone in juicy hunks. The preparation involves cooking the meat in advance, basting it in lots of olive oil and its own juices, and then reheating in a large clay oven for twenty minutes, with lots more basting immediately before serving in large portions. The Mauro restaurant, at the foot of the imposing castle at Peñafiel, only serves *cordero asado* and garnishing. A local red wine is the obvious choice, but anything from Rioja, Navarra or Valdepeñas will go extremely well.

NON-DO WINES

Castilla-León is the home to several single-estate vineyards where winemakers have been encouraged to make wines outside the DOs. Bodegas Mauro in Tudela de Duero immediately outside the DO of Ribera del Duero, is one that is producing excellent wines under the supervision of the former winemaker of Vega Sicilia. Nearby, at Sardon de Duero a superb investment of Novartis (a pharmaceuticals company in Barcelona) launched its first wines in 1998 under the name Abadía Retuerta; and a little further west are the ten hectares of Alta Pavina. Further north at Benavente, Bodegas Otero are establishing an excellent name for themselves with wines from Tempranillo, Mencía and Prieto Picudo.

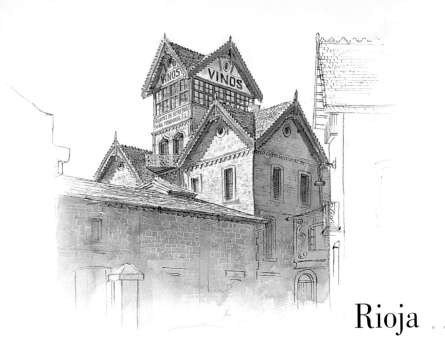

Rioja

It is not difficult to have a love affair with Rioja – I have had one for more than thirty years, not only with the wines, but with the region and its people.

One hundred kilometres south of Bilbao, the DOCa Rioja has vineyards in three provinces – La Rioja, Alava and Navarra, but predominantly La Rioja. The Sierras Cantabria and Demanda, in the west, embrace the region in a horseshoe that shelters the patchwork quilt of vineyards straddling the mighty River Ebro. It is very beautiful.

Rioja is the flagship wine region of Spain, and has evolved into the great and wealthy region it is today thanks to the persistent pursuit of better-quality wines and (something that may be of interest to those in advertising and marketing) the longest-running generic advertising and promotion campaign for wines.

The province is La Rioja; the wine area, just Rioja. The latter is divided into three zones – Rioja Alta, Rioja Alavesa and Rioja Baja, though the differentiation between these areas is diminishing as vineyard technology changes. The first two are higher in altitude, subject to Atlantic influences, and produce wines with finesse and balance from Tempranillo grapes. The more easterly Baja is lower and influenced by the warm, Mediterranean airflow that comes up the Ebro valley. The Baja produces larger quantities of softer, fatter wines from the Garnacha (Grenache in France) variety.

The quality of life here has improved greatly since Rioja wines became established beyond the shores of Spain, and many are experiencing unprecendented prosperity. Grape farmers saw their incomes treble between 1995 and 1998, and producers are having no difficulty selling every drop that is produced.

Momentarily, people thought Rioja would lose out to Ribera del Duero, but the reverse is happening, since the new region's emergence stimulated the Riojanos into greater efforts. The former trickle of ever better wines, young or aged, is turning into a torrent, making it difficult to keep up with developments. It seems that most are agreed that the long-term prosperity of Rioja lies with *Reserva* wines, examples of which are too many to mention.

There seems no reason why Rioja and Ribera del Duero cannot exist comfortably side by side, just as Bordeaux and Burgundy do in France. Rioja, like Bordeaux, after all is by far the larger.

TEMPRANILLO

Spain's most noble red variety is Tempranillo. Literally meaning 'early ripening', it is widely planted, and has been most closely associated with Rioja. However, its growing reputation on the world stage means that it is replacing former aliases like Tinto Fino in Ribera del Duero, Tinto de Toro in Toro, Cencibel in La Mancha, and Tinto de País or Tinto de Madrid in other parts of the centre. It has been suggested that not all are, in fact, Tempranillo, but the arguments are undermined by the increasing use of the name in these same regions, to the extent that Ull de Llebre in Cataluña has virtually disappeared.

The variety is known for its raspberry-scented, deep-coloured wines that are low in acidity, though they age well. Tempranillo benefits from being blended with small quantities of more complex varieties like Graciano or Cabernet Sauvignon.

LAGUARDIA

Of the many lovely towns in Rioja, this is one of the best. Perched on a hilltop at the foot of the Sierra Cantabria in Alava, its narrow, tidy, semi-pedestrianized streets are cool and quiet during a summer's day, but busy and alive when evening comes. In summer, the town balcony, with its splendid view to the west, is the preferred meeting point for the townsfolk as they watch the setting sun. The village is very popular with Bilbainans and Madrileños, who often spend weekends at one of the small but high-class hotels, visiting Bodegas like Palacio, Artadi or Campillo.

GRACIANO

A grape variety neglected for too long, especially by the Riojanos, and, even now, they are only paying lip service to it. Providing very small grapes and little juice, it has not been in favour, even though, when added to a blend it provides colour, aroma and acidity. In Rioja, I think they hope the more productive Cabernet Sauvignon, which has crept into the region, will prove a good substitute. By the way, it is highly unlikely that we shall ever see a pure Rioja Cabernet Sauvignon, since the vast majority are against such levelling of the region's reputation. Only one or two mavericks have even thought about it, and in the not too distant future I hope the regulating council will establish a law that states the variety has to be less than half the make-up of any Rioja wine.

MARQUES DE RISCAL

Marqués de Riscal, in Elciego, in the Rioja Alavesa, claim to be the first to have introduced Cabernet Sauvignon into Spain, during the mid-nineteenth century. Be that as it may, they have always enjoyed a special dispensation to use a small quantity of the fruit of this vine, although it is available to all for experimental purposes. Riscal produce *Reserva* reds and young *rosado* in Rioja, while their white wines come from Rueda.

OAK AGEING

This is a skill of which the Spaniards are justifiably proud, and which is identified most of all with Rioja. They have refined the system introduced by the Bordelaise, using it more as they do in the Rhône, by keeping the wines in barrels for longer.

Winemakers are free to age wines for as short a time, or as long as they wish, but there is legislation covering the three ageing classifications used on labels:

Crianza is for red wines aged for a minimum of six months in oak barrels (Rioja, Ribera del Duero, Navarra and others, require twelve months minimum). Bottle ageing is not mandatory but is being encouraged.

Reserva is for red wines aged for a minimum of one year in oak barrels and sold in their fourth year. However, Rioja and other regions now insist on a minimum of three years between barrel and bottle, with a minimum of one year in each.

Gran Reserva is for red wines aged a minimum of two years in oak barrels and three years in bottle.

In years gone by, some wines might have been aged for ten years or more, before bottling, and several great wines are still aged for longer than the minimums. Meanwhile, a number of new-style 'young' wines have been introduced with as little as three to six months in oak, though it is difficult to know this, because the regulating council does not allow this information to be put on the label – a bit daft, but that's legislation for you.

CAMPO VIEJO

The largest company in Rioja is Bodegas y Bebidas, who own the two largest Bodegas, namely Campo Viejo and Age, and sell over two million cases of Rioja every year. The B & B Group also own Bodegas in Navarra, La Mancha, Valdepeñas, Jumilla, Ribeiro, Rias Baixas and now Ribera del Duero. More familiar to the older amongst us as Savin, its influence on Spain's wine industry has been enormous.

TERROIR

In the simplest terms *terroir* means the unique conditions that exist in one vineyard or one small part of a vineyard, dictated by aspect, soil and the microclimatic conditions. Terroir is a preoccupation of Telmo Rodríguez, who has an unerring belief in the Spanish vineyards. A winemaker in the real sense, Telmo not only makes the outstanding Remelluri from the family estate at Labastida in Rioja, but a red and a *rosado* in Navarra and a white in Rueda. He is following these up with a traditional Málaga and a red from old vines in Toro, as well as other Riojas, and all based on the specific *terroir* he finds.

SINGLE ESTATES

In Rioja single estates are comparatively few, but increasing in number. Some notable ones are Baron de Oña (La Rioja Alta), Contino (Cune), Marqués de Murrieta, Marqués de Vargas and Remelluri. One that will steal the limelight as we go into the twenty-first century is Finca Valpiedra, completed just before the Millennium by the family of Martinéz Bujanda. It is a superb new Bodega in eighty hectares of vineyards in a loop on the south bank of the River Ebro, between Cenicero and Fuenmayor. All that has been done here embodies the commitment of Riojanos to their future.

RED PEPPERS

These are a delicacy of Rioja and Navarra. *Pimientos Rojo a la Brasa* (red peppers cooked on a charcoal grill) are sweet, piquant and delicious. Don't fall for the question as to whether you want them hot (piquant) or mild, because nobody can identify the difference with any conviction. In autumn a common sight is ladies roasting peppers over braziers in the street, before removing the skins and bottling them in garlic and olive oil.

THE BATTLE OF WINE

A Rioja fiesta is the Battle of Wine, at which the sole objective seems to be to see how much red wine one can throw, spray, or pour over others. It's a pretty pointless exercise, and one that does not help the good image of Rioja any more than spraying Champagne on Grand Prix podia helps the image of that wine.

MARQUÉS DE CÁCERES

Probably the best-known international brand in Rioja is Marqués de Cáceres, at Cenicero in Rioja Alta, which was founded by a Frenchman, Henri Forner, in 1970 and was an instant success, not only for a magnificent range of reds, but for some very innovative white wines. Unquestionably the success they are achieving worldwide owes a lot to the very distinctive and smart packaging.

Navarra

        The province of Navarra is the oldest independent region of Spain, and stretched to Bordeaux and Barcelona in the Middle Ages. It has held a special status in Spain for several centuries, being allowed to raise and account for its own taxes long before other regions. Navarra is acclaimed for its verdant landscape, abundance of flowers, fruit and vegetables, and the bright and friendly people. It was a favourite visiting place for Ernest Hemingway, whose love for Navarra manifested itself in his books based on time spent in Pamplona, especially every July at the running of the bulls during the fiesta of San Fermin.

Navarra has always been an important wine region with strong traces of the Roman influence of two thousand years ago. Dismissed, until recently, as the poor man's Rioja, the DO has established an identity of its own by concentrating on a selection of indigenous and foreign varietals to complement the best of the traditional oak-aged wines. Tempranillo, Cabernet Sauvignon, Merlot and Muscatel have all succeeded in Navarra, but most notable of all, to date, has been the success with Chardonnay. The New World was stunned when a Navarra

Bodega won the trophy for Chardonnay at the prestigious International Wine Challenge in London, a few years ago.

EVENA

The producers owe a lot of their success to an exceptional initiative of the regional government, which established an oenological and experimental station in an old Distillery at Olite. Called Evena, it is devoted to examining and advising on every aspect of the soil, climate, vines, grapes – skins, pips and flesh – wines, casks and equipment. They have experimental vineyards, superbly equipped laboratories, tasting rooms and seminar facilities, where they hold regular conferences and education programmes. The original head of the experimental side of Evena – Javier Ochoa – now produces superb wines at his own Bodega just outside the town.

CHARDONNAY

Winemakers in Navarra and, more recently, in high Cataluña have produced top wines from the Chardonnay vine, not least the unoaked ones, which I must admit I find more subtle and attractive. One detects

a disenchantment with Chardonnay in Spain because the producers are unhappy with making the same wine as so many others around the world. Now they know they can match the best they want to work with their own varieties as far as possible, and I think it is unlikely this variety will establish a much more substantial presence.

Having said that, I read of an Australian commentator who complained about the plethora of boring unoaked Chardonnays in his country. My riposte would be that there is a surfeit of barrel-fermented and oak-aged Chardonnays in Europe and a well-made, fresh unoaked Chardonnay of the year is often better. If you do not believe me try the Gran Feudo of Julian Chivite or the Bach Chardonnay of Penedés.

MENESTRA DE VERDURAS DEL TIEMPO

This dish is not unique to Navarra, but must have originated here because of the abundance of naturally grown vegetables. It is a dish of lightly boiled vegetables in season, which are then lightly stir-fried very briefly with a little olive oil, before being served in extremely generous portions. Most cooks add a little chopped serrano ham, but I think that should be discouraged. A young, chilled *rosado* goes very well with this dish.

SEÑORIOS

These are normally private estates, but not necessarily producing wine. However, the Señorio de Arinzano at Estella, belonging to the family company Bodegas Julian Chivite, famous for their Gran Feudo range, is entirely devoted to the vine. The 200 hectares of immaculate vineyards are the source of superb Reserva red wines and a very special late picked Muscat Petits Grains all sold under the Colección 125 label.

Another special Señorio in Navarra is that of Sarria just outside Puente la Reina, where in a self-contained environment, vineyards rub shoulders with livestock and fruit farming, and the grape pickers and wild boar compete as to who gets the grapes first.

Aragón

Some people have described Aragón as cowboy country and one can see what they mean when observing the large areas of arid land and steep escarpments. However, cowhands would find little work here because wheatlands, fruit orchards and vineyards are the most important agricultural activities.

For a long time I found it difficult to come to terms with Aragón, but the more I know it the more I am drawn there. The climate is harsh, rainfall low, temperatures extreme and, in the north, the cold winter winds blow almost incessantly. The seemingly unending, and boring motorway from Rioja to Cataluña gave me a misleading first impression, and since exploring the Ebro valley vineyards and the Pyrenean foothills, I have found a warmth behind the toughness of the land and its people.

The contrasts in the beauty of the Odessa Nature Reserve in the Pyrenees, and the rich vegetative Cinca valley, or the central plateau and truffle-littered forests of Teruel are among the greater qualities of Aragón. In the middle is the historical and wealthy capital city of Zaragoza, which links Madrid in the south and the Basque country to the west, with Cataluña to the east.

ARAGÓN

SOMONTANO

The wine region that occupies just 1,800 hectares of vineyards in the
rocky, inhospitable landscape of the beautiful Pyrenean foothills is
Somontano, where wines of arresting interest are being produced. It
is the wine region that concentrated outsiders' interest in the wines of
Aragón, when new minds focused on the varieties introduced by the
French family of Lalanne from their own country 100 years ago. Three
others, Enate, Pirineos and Viñas del Vero have taken the region
forward with wines that have surprised just about everybody with their
intensity of fruit and style.

Most unusual of these French varieties are the two white grapes
of Gewürztraminer and Chenin Blanc, which are little used elsewhere
in Spain.

GEWÜRZTRAMINER

The lovely spicy grape variety of Alsace with orange blossom aromas
is scarce in Spain, but it provides attractive wines in cooler areas like
Somontano and Bierzo.

CALATAYUD

In the southern mountains of Zaragoza province on the river Jalón, Calatayud was for a long time better known for historical reasons than for its wines. It is foreign winemakers, British-based especially, who have realized the potential by identifying good raw materials in the vineyards (especially older Garnacha vines), and finding suitable Bodegas. They have introduced new technology and skills with the aim of improving what is already there, rather than making wines to their own formula.

It was at the old Co-operative San Gregorio, in Calatayud, on a bitterly cold day that I witnessed just what can be achieved. It must have been one of the coldest tastings on record, but I easily understood why they are having difficulty keeping up with demand. All these wines have been going to Northern Europe, but if one Madrileño who passes regularly on trips to and from Zaragoza is prepared to divert to buy the 'English wine', whither the consignments of the future?

CARIÑENA

This is both a grape variety (Carignan in French) and a wine region, where, ironically, the grape variety does not dominate; instead it is the Garnacha. The DO is next to, and east of Calatayud, and was famous for two things: the natural very high-strength wines that were widely used for blending both in and outside Spain; and the village of Fuentetodos, the birthplace of Goya. Foreign winemakers are bringing their skills here too, with most of the wines being shipped to Britain, Germany and Scandinavia.

VIURA (MACABEO)

This variety is chosen for its adaptability rather than its potential. Prevalent in the north of Spain (Cataluña, Aragón, Navarra and Rioja), it is being introduced in the south. It blends quite well with Aíren, but the end result is not especially arresting, and although a few producers have made notable wines with pure Viura, its best attribute is as a vehicle for the vanillin flavours of oak, such as Rioja *Crianza* whites.

VINOS DE LA TIERRA

In Aragón *Vinos de la Tierra* are important, numbering six in all. Now that wines from this autonomy are being taken much more seriously, we can expect to hear more about these lesser-known ones. One that has come to notice is called Domus, produced from Cabernet Sauvignon and Garnacha and scoring very high marks in tasting competitions. It is made by Venta d'Aubert in Teruel.

Cataluña

Cataluña (or Catalunya in Catalan) is the autonomous region of north-eastern Spain. It is blessed with an abundance of wines, having nine Denominations of Origin, plus 95 per cent of Cava production. It is one of the most active and hard-working areas of Spain, centred around the international city of Barcelona on the motorway that now extends from Copenhagen to Almería. Goodness knows how many visitors to Spain pass through Cataluña in the course of a year but it must be a huge number. In late 1999 the Denomination of Origin Catalunya was introduced to embrace all those vineyards not within the existing smaller nine DOs. It is the first effort in Spain to bring a little more flexibility to their wine regulations by introducing an overall category rather as exists in Bordeaux. So, expect to see this name appearing on labels as of now.

I seldom think of coastal Cataluña as beautiful, except the northern end of the Costa Brava, but the wines are a different story. Though the temperate, Mediterranean climate can be difficult when producing the best-quality wines, new technology in both vineyard and Bodega, along with moving vineyards higher into the hills, is making it easier.

COSTERS DEL SEGRE

This DO evolved from the creation of the Raimat estate, near Lerida is Costers del Segre. It is a harsh environment of cold dry winds in winter, and very hot even drier summers, yet several Bodegas are producing classy wines to match those emanating from the founder company.

The original estate was founded in 1900 by the Raventos family of Codorníu. It occupies 3,000 hectares of bleak yet arable land irrigated by the Segre canal that crosses the province. Codorníu have established a mixed agricultural domaine, of which half is planted with vines, both indigenous and foreign. Their strong resources have allowed them to experiment extensively with all sorts of technology, especially in the vineyards, from soil evaluation through training of the vines and canopy management. This detailed research led them to launching some of the first single-variety wines in Spain and, more recently, to introducing three *Pago* wines.

PAGO

This is the prefix often given to a wine made from grapes grown in a single vineyard, or part of a vineyard, where the topography, soil properties and microclimatic conditions are the same for each vine from which the wine is made. This evaluation enters into the realms of *terroir*, which is not a subject to tackle in this book, but it does mean that the resulting wine should be exceptional in quality. If it is not, it's hardly worth embarking on the exercise in the first place.

CABERNET SAUVIGNON

The Cabernet Sauvignon grape has established itself extremely well in Spain, but is distinct from the same variety in most other countries. It takes on softer, more attractive and less astringent characteristics, and the blackcurrant aromas and flavours are not always quite so obvious, but it adds structure and acidity when used in blends. Indeed, the match of Cabernet Sauvignon with Tempranillo is as near a perfect match as any parent could wish their children to make.

ALELLA

A tiny DO in the northern suburbs of Barcelona is Alella, which contains three producers, including the inevitable Co-operative. However, it is the other two – Marqués de Alella and Roura – that have established this tiny region, mainly with white wines, but with red and *rosados* too. It has been their success with the Pansa Blanca that has been most notable, both for still wines and Cava, of which Parxet is a classic example.

PANSA BLANCA (XAREL-LO)

This flavoursome but subtle-tasting grape makes excellent light, crisp, still wine, and first-class Cava, either on its own, or as a component part with Macabeo and Parellada.

PENEDES

To the south-west of Barcelona, Penedés is a large region producing prolific quantities of mainly white wines. The moving of vineyards to higher ground, where the vines can benefit from the cooler influences, has resulted in subtler wines with more finesse and style. Penedés is also gaining recognition for a number of stylish red wines of international standing, produced both from indigenous and several of the foreign varieties.

There is constant confusion in this region, because the main centre of production for Cava is located at San Sadurni de Noya in the heart of the zone, and the buying power of the Cava houses for grapes has been dominant for a long time. The fact that they are now having to compete with even more winemakers is good for all of us because the quality can only get even better.

MIGUEL TORRES

This is the name most identified with modern winemaking in Spain. Don Miguel Torres Carbo, late father of the current President of the company, Don Miguel Agustin Torres, was a single-minded and powerful personality. He established his strategy of producing the very best wines to sell in the best restaurants of the world. Today it makes

sense, but at the time, most of us would have said he was mad. The family Bodega was bombed during the Civil War, but rebuilt immediately, and when Europe opened up for business after the 1939–45 conflict, he set off with his equally determined wife, Doña Margarita, in a small unheated car to visit these restaurants and sell his wines.

Later, his son Miguel Agustin went to wine school in France, and with his return, the Torres' part in the wine revolution really began. Torres became singularly identified with good-quality Spanish wines, and was probably the first with stainless steel and temperature-controlled fermentation. He questioned every established tenet in winemaking, and was experimenting in the vineyards long before many in the New World. What he had learnt in France did not necessarily apply further south, in those days, and everything needed to be checked.

It might also be said that he is the pioneer of the revival of the Chilean wine industry, after investing in a winery and vineyards there in 1979. Since then the company has set up the Marimar Torres winery in California, and is starting to plant in the Hebei province of China.

PINOT NOIR

It is generally agreed that Pinot Noir is a difficult variety that does not take to any habitat with ease, and although there are a few good examples in Spain, results are erratic. Its variously strawberry, raspberry and plummy characteristics explain why the Tempranillo is sometimes thought to be related to it. Its frustrating irregularity of performance has meant few have the courage to employ it, but Torres' Mas Borras, on its day, is a lovely plummy wine, while Viñas del Vero have had success with Val de Luga in Somontano.

CATALAN GASTRONOMY

Wide ranging is the way to describe Catalan gastronomy. Although most of the best seafood now comes from the Atlantic, Barcelona (along with Madrid) is one of the few places where you will find good shellfish and fish: the seafood restaurants at the Porto Olimpico are

tremendous. Those who have heard of it will want to visit Los Caracoles off the bottom of the Ramblas – great fun, decent food, a good selection of wines, cheerful staff and Tuna Bands (singers with guitars and banjos) from the University to liven up the evening. The French subculture means there are wonderful breads and patisserie and excellent beef. Don't be put off by those Catalan dishes that mix fish and meat with sauces that sometimes contain chocolate – they are, in fact, extremely tasty. Lamb and lobster, or rabbit and crab are among the best, and there is always plenty of good wine to wash them down.

MERLOT

The classic Bordeaux variety has taken to Spain like a duck to water, both for red and *rosado*, and particularly in Cataluña. Its cassis-like jammy softness is extremely appealing and gives the pinks more than usual personality.

MONISTROL

The name of a charming small village outside San Sadurni, which has a Bodega named after the Marqués of the same name. It lies in a lovely setting surrounded by 300 hectares of immaculate vineyards of its own. A subsidiary of Arco Bodegas Unidas, it produces nearly twelve million bottles of Penedés and Cava wines a year. The Bodega is a delightful combination of the old original buildings and more recent additions.

PRIORATO

I would rather not let people into the secret of this place, but they are making superb wines, so I have to mention it. It must be one of the

very few enclaves anywhere where there is real tranquillity. Some
seventy kilometres inland from Tarragona city, and surrounded by an
imposing escarpment of granite, Priorato is small, harsh and
inhospitable, yet it is strangely beautiful, blessed with a dry and
temperate climate.

The cultivation of the vine is tortuous, with plants on small, steep,
labour-intensive terraces, and production (even from young vines) is
very low – such that one wonders what drives them to do it. However,
when you see the superb fruit they gather from the old Garnacha vines,
and taste wines with huge intensity and richness, you realize that

maybe they are not so crazy after all. Believe it or not, the two people, Rene Barbier (Clos Mogador) and Alvaro Palacios (Finca Dofí), who set Priorato on the road to success, were working in Rioja before arriving here.

GARNACHA

This grape originated in Spain and flourished because of the abundant harvest it produces for *rosados* and young reds. Treated with some contempt, because its value was misunderstood, it has been highly sought after since winemakers discovered the wonderful spicy fruit of the old vines for making rich resonant wines. Priorato is a prime example, but there are others. Martínez Bujanda, producers in Rioja, have confounded critics of the variety by making an outstanding wine from pure Garnacha, aged in oak for three years.

CAPÇANES

Capçanes is a small village in a beautiful setting near Falset in the DO Tarragona. They believe they should be part of Priorato, but the terrain and climate is different enough for others to disagree. Nevertheless, the Co-operative there is making stunning wines from old Garnacha and Cariñena, with some Tempranillo, Cabernet Sauvignon, Merlot and Syrah. Remarkable, among a remarkable range of wines, is the nearly impossible-to-buy Pansal de Calas sweet Garnacha, which is ideal with Christmas pudding and chocolate desserts.

SCALA DEI

For so long Scala Dei was the only Bodega the outside world associated with Priorato. It is part of a twelfth-century monastery in a secluded hamlet at the foot of the escarpment, and Murray and I have a lasting memory of peace and calm while we waited for the right light. In three hours all we saw were two cars, and all we heard was the light breeze in the trees, the occasional bird, and the chiming of a grandfather clock. Oh and they make great wines too.

Mallorca

The wines of this holiday island and émigré paradise have shown a marked improvement in the short time I have lived here. This is pure coincidence but good to witness, especially as many visitors prefer to drink the local wines, even when they are more expensive than those from the mainland.

At the beginning of the twentieth century there were 40,000 hectares of vineyards on the island, but the Phylloxera bug came and, as in the rest of Europe, devastated the vineyards. Not wishing to buy the immune Californian rootstock on to which most vines are grafted these days, the farmers opted for almond and olive trees instead, the former proving to be a great success.

BINISSALEM

Vineyards now total around 1,500 hectares and only 300 of these are in the Denomination of Binissalem in the centre of the island. The DO is dominated by Franja Roja, belonging to the family of José Ferrer, but they are leading the way and have invested large sums in a new fermentation plant and ageing facilities.

VINOS DE LA TIERRA

The Pla de Levant, on the south of the island, are several small wineries making some excellent *Vinos de la Tierra* from indigenous and foreign vine varieties: dry Muscat, Cabernet Sauvignon, Pinot Noir, Merlot and Chardonnay. The region is expected to be a DO by the year 2001. Two expert friends of mine quite independently described one particular Chardonnay as among the best they had ever tasted. No, I am not telling you who makes it – he makes only 1,000 bottles a year, and it is expensive enough already.

Hardly any Mallorca wines are exported because they can sell them in the Balearic islands at better prices.

MANTO NEGRO

A red vine variety probably unique to the Balearic islands, Manto Negro is mandatory to a quite high percentage of vines in Binissalem. The resulting wine is middle-weight and lightly aromatic, with firm, dark berry flavours, and it ages well in cask.

The Levante

This is that part of Spain from Castejón through Valencia and Alicante to Murcia in the extreme south-east corner. It is where south meets north, where Andalucian meets Catalan, and, for me, the friendly and welcoming atmosphere is as warm as you could hope to find. Valencia is a beautiful city on which they have lavished care and attention with extensive renovations, while, along with Alicante, it is reputed to have the most temperate of climates in the western Mediterranean.

In agricultural terms vines are hugely important, while the region is also home to almonds in the north, citrus and rice in the centre, and date palms, melons, peaches and artichokes in the south.

VALENCIA

This name refers to a province, a city and a wine region; not a very big one, but well-known because of substantial companies like Gandía and Schenk, and the huge amounts of wine that are still shipped from the port. The wines are more white than red, and Valencia Moscatels have established a good reputation.

MOSCATEL (MUSCAT AND MUSCATEL)

A generic term for a wide range of varieties of this sweet-wine-producing grape. Perhaps one of its greatest features is that the wines taste like ripe grapes, an increasingly uncommon anomaly when describing the different aromas and flavours of wines.

Even the technical books on the subject are uncertain about the particular clones of the vine that are used around the regions. In Valencia and Alicante, it is Moscatel Alejandria, of Egyptian origin, which probably came with the Phoenicians when they landed in Andalucia. It is pretty clear that Málaga Moscatel (Málaga), Moscatel Gordo Blanco (Jerez), and Moscatel Romano (Tarragona and Penedés) are all the same variety. It is also found in Mallorca where Miguel Oliver is producing a very attractive, and widely acclaimed dry Muscat.

UTIEL-REQUENA

The region of Utiel-Requena is totally dependent on the vine and ancillary trades. The size and concentration of vineyards are amazing, and the potential breathtaking. The red vine dominates, the Bobal variety occupying four fifths of the total vineyards, but it used to be more than 95 per cent, until they started replacing large areas with Tempranillo and foreign varieties. Hoyo Valley, Murviedro and Torre Oria are making some splendid wines, which are being widely sold, but 40,000 hectares produce an awful lot of wine and there is a long way to go.

BOBAL

This is the predominant red grape variety in Utiel-Requena. On the face of it, the wine is fairly lean with good acidity, but yields beefy-coloured reds and good *rosados*, which go well with local rice dishes.

PAELLA

Despite the fact that expert cooks consider paella as a gastronomically excellent *cocina*, it has been so debased that many people cannot take it seriously. It originated in Valencia and Alicante and was the staple diet of the farmworkers in the *Huerta* (market garden) and often accompanied by *rosado*.

The word *paella* is, in fact, the name given to the pan in which the rice dish is cooked, so the correct name for rice cooked this way, is *Arroz a la Paella*. The original version is rice of the region, with lamb, rabbit and a few green beans and peas. Of course, things have changed and there are mixed and seafood versions. In Alicante the speciality is *Arroz Abanda*, which is the rice cooked in stock and served alone. But beware – sometimes, after you have stuffed yourself with the rice, they bring another dish of all the cooked ingredients for you to eat.

DOBLE PASTA

This is an intensely full-bodied red wine that is enjoying a revival in winemaking, as producers seek to extract the maximum from their grapes. You will have read elsewhere in this book (p.27) of how *rosados* are made from the first free-run juice of the grapes, after a very short time with the skins. There remains a substantial amount of potentially good must, so, rather than press this *pasta*, the producer then adds more grapes to create a darker, heavier wine, with more alcohol that he can then use for blending. Hence *Doble Pasta*, or two pastas.

ALICANTE

Alicante is a diverse wine region with little individual identity, except for Moscatels, but some excellent ones. Notable among them is the *Cosecha Miel* (Honey Harvest) of Felipe Gutierrez de la Vega, made from Moscatel Alexandria at Parcent, inland from Calpe on the Costa Blanca. Just south, at Alfa de Pi, near Benidorm, is Enrique Mendoza, where José (the son) is making a range of red imported varieties that are excellent and winning gold medals, almost every one. The vineyards are eighty kilometres inland, at Villena, high up in the mountains.

SYRAH (SHIRAZ)

This is a grape that has been overlooked for too long, which is surprising for a variety from a continental climate similar to that of the Rhône. The few producers – like Mendoza, Manzaneque and Griñon – that are making wines with Syrah are receiving acclaim from many experts, and it certainly has a great future.

FONDILLON

Sometimes called the Port wine of the Levante, *Fondillón* is a bit of an enigma. Nobody seems to agree as to exactly how it is made, but it is quite different to that of Portugal. In essence, it is a product of Monastrell (Mourvèdre in France) grapes with high, natural alcoholic strength (between 16 and 18 per cent) that is aged in oak vats or barrels for anything between ten and twenty years, and it may be dry or partially sweet. The examples I have tasted are not unattractive, but essentially for warming the cockles in cold weather.

MURCIA

The most southerly part of the Levante is Murcia, the heart of Spain's market garden in the driest corner of the country. The Moors installed an extensive and sophisticated irrigation system, much of which is still in use, but the two main wine regions of Jumilla and Yecla did not benefit from its introduction, being too far away in the mountains. Even the vine struggles to survive in these areas, not that this is always a bad thing, because a little stress for the vine helps yield better-quality fruit.

Jumilla and Yecla

These are neighbouring Denominations, Jumilla being ten times the size of Yecla. One of the producers laments, 'There is no reason to come here, unless you are in a business to do with wine' and, sadly, he is right. Ninety kilometres due west of Alicante, the landscape is unattractive and a dreary brown, but there is a good reason to visit: the Monastrell vine. It represents over 90 per cent of the 45,000 hectares of vineyards, and only now is the real potential showing, as post and wire training with drip irrigation is slowly introduced. Agapito Rico was one of the first to hit the headlines with Carchelo, but he planned to age it all in oak until Stephen Metzler, a Seattle wine merchant, came along and insisted on purchasing the deep-coloured, intensely fruity wine without ageing. It was instantly successful in the United States. Meantime, in Yecla Bodegas Castaño are winning gold medals with several of their wines, not least the single varietal of Monastrell produced with the help of the Australian winemaker Dave Morrison.

Monastrell

Known as Mourvèdre in France, Monastrell is the second-most-planted red variety in Spain, after Garnacha. Known, also, as Morastell in Cataluña, and Moristel in Aragón, it ripens late, so performs best in lower and warmer areas, has high sugar levels, good structure and gamey aromas with blackberry flavours.

Don Simon

This is a name you will see on trucks all over the country. It is a brand of table wines and fruit juices widely sold for daily use in Spanish households. Changing fashion has led J. Garcia Carrion, the producers (who are based in Jumilla), to cast their net wider into DOs such as Cava, Penedés, Rioja and Ribera del Duero. One can expect an already powerful force in the industry to get even stronger.

Andalucia and
The Canary Islands

The images of the romantic south are almost everybody's first impression of this contrasting country. Bright blue skies, golden sandy beaches, white towns, cool patios, flamenco dancers, the list is endless, but they all flit across the mind. And let us not forget the glorious, Moorish cities such as Sevilla, Córdoba and Granada, which probably evoke even more powerful memories.

My first visit to the south was to Jerez de la Frontera in 1957, when I saw such a different country. In the poorer towns children wore either shorts or a shirt but seldom both, and hardly ever shoes. Families lived in one room with the bed, kitchen and sanitation all together, but the warmth and friendliness of everybody was overwhelming, and with Sherry at two pesetas *acopita*, life's pleasures came cheap to the lucky ones like me.

JEREZ-XÉRÈS-SHERRY

Jerez-Xérès-Sherry y Manzanilla-Sanlucar de Barrameda, or, in a word Sherry. I have to be careful I do not eulogize too much about this wonderful wine, but it is the real thing, and let any pretenders to the throne think up their own name and not ride on the back of Sherry from Spain.

The Sherry Triangle, within which the best vineyards are located, is formed by the three towns of Jerez de la Frontera, Puerto de Santa Maria and Sanlucar de Barrameda in the province of Cádiz. There are three types of vines: the all-important Palomino, Moscatel Gordo Blanco and a reducing area of Pedro Ximénez (otherwise known as PX).

BUTTS

The large oak casks used in Jerez for ageing the wine are known as butts. At 500 litres, they are more than double the size of light wine barrels, but since they remain in their stacks for many years, the handling problems of such large casks are less. At the Las Copas Bodega of González Byass, it is not unusual to see Whisky casks being aged and coloured with Sherry, before the casks are removed, broken down into bundles, and shipped off to Scotland for reassembly and used for ageing some Malts.

THE SHERRY PRODUCTION PROCESS

Palomino yields, in the first instance, two wines – Fino and Oloroso – or to be more precise, a single wine with different characteristics, which are determined about four or five months after the vintage. Once the tasters have classified the wines into one of the two categories, they are put into a 'nursery' to await allocation to the Soleras, the unique ageing system. Both these wines are dry and will remain so until they are prepared for bottling and despatch to the customer.

The Fino wine is left as it is, and a bacteria *flor* is allowed to grow on the surface of the wine. This keeps the air out, and the wine very pale and light in texture, and will continue for some ten or more years. When the *flor* dies, the air can reach the surface of the wine and it takes on colour and a nutty flavour. This becomes a genuine Amontillado (see below), still absolutely dry, but very expensive.

The Oloroso wine, however, has wine alcohol added to it to prevent the bacteria growing, so that it will take on colour more quickly and develop into a golden brown wine, to be sold dry, or sweet, depending on the customer's requirements.

The Moscatel and Pedro Ximénez (PX) are picked late and dried on mats in the sun to turn them into raisins, which results in intensely rich, sweet wines, essentially for blending but which are jolly good liqueurs too.

THE TYPES OF SHERRY

The greatest skills of the Sherry winemaker are the ability to taste the finest nuances and blend wines to match samples of the customers' requirements. Although there are only two basic styles and the sweet wine, there are several categories of Sherry that can be purchased, the following five of which are most frequently found:

Fino is a delicate, light, dry wine fortified to about 15.5 per cent of alcohol. It should be drunk chilled and as young as possible. Once open, it will keep fresh in the refrigerator for a few days. Finos vary depending on which town they are from, so you can choose from Jerez Fino, Puerto Fino and Manzanilla-Sanlucar de Barrameda. Those from Jerez are the most robust, while those from Puerto fall between Jerez and Manzanilla.

Amontillado: I have described the purest kind of Amontillado above (under The Sherry Production Process), but cost makes it prohibitive for the normal commercial market. Thus, Fino and Oloroso are blended, and perhaps a quantity of one of the sweeter wines added to make it a fortified, medium-dry wine at about 16.5 per cent.

Oloroso Dry is a rich, warm, nutty wine that is a splendid substitute for spirits as an aperitif, or served with some types of cheese. The best are about 18 per cent of alcohol. I recommend it in winter.

Cream, as in Bristol Cream, is an Oloroso blended with PX, and fortified to 17 or 18 per cent of alcohol.

Pale Cream is the result of a successful marketing ploy by Croft in the late 1960s, based on the theory that Fino is smart, but sweet is what they want.

The Sherry exporters are running a Sherry and ice campaign, and Sherry on the Rocks is a thoroughly good way to drink it, whatever the style.

THE SOLERA SYSTEM

The secret that ensures Sherry has a continuity of quality, style and character that never varies is the Solera System. This blending and ageing system is made up of several stages, in each of which there are the same number of butts. There is no stipulated limit to the number of stages, but four to six is average.

The oldest stage is the *solera* stage. When wine is sold from this stage, the butts are topped up with wine from the next-oldest stage (called a *criadera*), and that wine is topped up with wine from the next-oldest and so on. Each time wine is taken from butts in the same stage, it is blended together before being redistributed into the next-oldest stage. No more than 35 per cent of the wine can be removed from any butt in the Solera during a year, which means that the older wine passes its characteristics on to the younger wine. All these aspects are components in fufilling the purpose of this time-consuming but invaluable system.

THE COPITA

The classic glass they use for drinking Sherry in Jerez is the *copita*, and it is a far better glass than many, especially those stupid little schooners and other glasses that people in Britain fill to the brim. Wine glasses should be generous so that the wine can breathe and project the aromas of the wine. In fact, I prefer a larger glass than the *copita* for drinking Sherry: it is a tasting glass and is much the same shape but about twice the size.

SHERRY BARONS

We have heard about the British and Irish invaders of the late eighteenth century, who built the modern Sherry trade. Well, they built a very successful business, which created extremely rich families, and, when I first went down there, such wealth anywhere in Europe was rare. Among the large companies, GonzálezByass, Osborne and Caballero still have strong family ties, and manage to preserve their personalities in a harsher and more competitive world and with names like Valdespino, Hidalgo and Barbadillo also preserve the romantic tradition. On the other hand Croft, Domecq, Garvey, Sandeman and Williams and Humbert all belong to multinational conglomerates with the inevitable loss of identity. They all once enjoyed a magical lifestyle that we can only dream about now.

PALOMINO (LISTÁN BLANCO)

Palomino, unquestionably, the key vine variety for producing Sherry. However, it makes dull, characterless, light white wines and, fortunately, is being kicked out of Galicia and Rueda, where it was widely used until a few years ago. Long may it stay in Jerez, its original habitat.

FLAMENCO

This is, of course, the emotive dance and music of Andalucia with a confused profusion of origins. The roots of the art are multinational and multidoctrinal, being Arabic, Jewish, Visigoth, Gregorian and

Byzantine. Flamenco was originally sung and danced with only rythmic percussion as accompaniment until, early in the nineteenth century, the guitar was adopted.

The modern Flamenco of Andalucia is most classically practised in Jerez and Cádiz, followed by Sevilla, Córdoba and Granada. It is an emotional art depicting the extremes of love and hate, joy and sadness, jealousy and hope, and is not all foot-banging and hand-clapping as some might think. Of course, these aspects are an important part of its rythmic nature, though some of the most beautiful pieces are more in the way of ballet.

There is nothing like sitting in a smoky, dimly lit bar in the old quarter of an Andalucian town with a bottle of Sherry and a Flamenco group to experience the true depths of feelings the art conveys.

TAPAS

The word *tapa* means a cap, or lid, and its origins go back to one particular bar-owner's idea of putting a little saucer on top of a glass of wine to keep the flies out. But an empty saucer looked mean and inhospitable, so he put small cubes of cheese or an olive on it and, lo and behold, the flies returned. But from this small beginning the tapas culture was born. And it is very much a culture, which can only be fully appreciated when experienced in Spain.

The custom originated in Jerez but spread to other parts of Andalucia, Madrid and Valencia, in particular. Nowadays, you will find first-class tapas bars in every corner of Spain, as well as in other countries.

A *tapa* is really a mouthful, while a *ración* is more like a starter portion, but these days the word tapas covers both meanings. Some tapas are very simple, but others require the expertise of a good chef in their preparation and can be quite expensive. I love this form of eating for its informality and element of fun, especially with a good bottle of wine.

MONTILLA

Lying in the hottest part of Spain, in Córdoba province, is Montilla. The Denomination has long been subjugated to Jerez, which still has a special dispensation to buy the intensely sweet Pedro Ximénez wine there. But the wines of Montilla are both similar and quite different. The vine is the Pedro Ximénez (PX), not Palomino, and the natural alcoholic strength is much higher. Indeed Montilla wines are usually over 15 per cent, and they also use the Solera System, as in Jerez. Montilla sells as much wine as Jerez in Spain, but less in export markets, though the wines are popular in Holland and Britain. The two leading producers are Alvear and Pérez Barquero, both of whom are prominent in the export markets.

PEDRO XIMÉNEZ (PX)

This is the dominant vine variety in Montilla, is also important in Málaga, and has limited plantings in Jerez. Famous for the intensely sweet wines it yields, after the grapes are dried to raisins on mats in the sun, it produces excellent dry wines in Montilla, where, like the Palomino in Jerez, it is most suited. Legend has it that a soldier of the same name brought the vine back from the campaigns in the Netherlands in the seventeenth century.

PLATEROS BARS

Unique to Córdoba, plateros bars were established in the Jewish Quarter at the end of the nineteenth century, by Silversmiths who were finding trade tough. They lived in classical Andalucian houses with lovely cool patios and turned the ground floor into tapas bars serving Montilla wines produced at their own Bodega in the city.

MÁLAGA WINES

These were known in Victorian Britain as Mountain Wine, because the vines are grown on the steep slopes behind the city. The grapes are Pedro Ximénez and Moscatel, and before being pressed they are dried in the sun, in troughs (*lagares*). The fermentation is stopped with the addition of wine alcohol, rather as they do with Port. The wine is then delivered to the Bodegas in the city, where, by law, Málaga wines have to be aged and blended.

These wines have experienced a decline in popularity in recent years, which is a pity because they are excellent postprandial wines.

THE CANARIES

The Canary Islands get their name from the old Spanish name for the dogs (*canos*) that they found on the islands when they invaded during the fifteenth century. The little yellow birds, in turn, get their name from the islands. When I was asked to write a report three years ago, I was astonished to find there were eight Denominations of Origin in the Canaries. Today there are nine and the figure will soon be ten. I was just as surprised, when I got to the islands, to find them struggling with volcanic rock, humidity and very low yields. But, when told they sold everything in the islands at higher prices than much better wines from the mainland, I shrugged and got on with my job.

Making the report allowed me to visit five of the islands, and it was both interesting and rewarding. On a more recent visit, it was gratifying to find they had obviously taken note of one of the most important recommendations, although, to my distress, they ignored the others.

In the past the vines are either trailed on the volcanic rock or propped very near to the ground with abundant foliage, so that, in both cases, the bunches of grapes could not ripen properly. Believe it or not, in this idyllic holiday environment, they have a problem with light in the vineyards, because of the humid clouds that hang on the mountain peaks, and there were obvious benefits to be gained from training the vines on posts and wires with drip irrigation. I was delighted to note that this is mandatory in the newest DO of Monte-Lentiscal, in Gran Canaria, but, by contrast, the fact that they are still planting Listán Blanco (Palomino) vines is heartbreaking.

There are few good wines in the Canaries, except the reds and *rosados* of Viña Norte and Monje of Tacoronte-Acentejo in Tenerife, some whites from Mozaga and El Grifo in Lanzarote, and several superb sweet Moscatels and Malvasías in La Palma and El Hierro.

MALVASIA

This is a variety that suffers from being a low-yielding type, yet it produces delicately flavoured wines. Thought to be one of the oldest varieties, and recognized for good sweet wines, not least in the Canary Islands, it has been much neglected.

Castilla La Mancha
and Madrid

It is odd how countryside that is flat virtually without relief can attract one with its simplicity, especially for those like me who love mountains. The enormous southern plateau of Castilla La Mancha has that effect, with its seemingly endless sea of vines. In winter the reddish and dark brown earth, with row upon row of heavily pruned vine stubs and scattered little white buildings, is a picture that immediately comes to mind. The famous windmills are not as much in evidence as one might expect apart from at Campo de Criptana, Mota del Cuervo or Consuegra, but the great distances of uninterrupted landscape, where shelter is scarce from the biting winds or unrelenting sun, leave a lasting memory.

La Mancha (Manxa, or scorched earth to the Moors) was described by Miguel de Cervantes, the author of *Don Quixote*, as having a climate of *nueve meses de invierno, y tres meses de inferno* (nine months of winter and three months of infernal heat). It is a pretty apt summary. The people are hard-working and materially poor, scratching a living from vines, a few other crops, shepherding or a support business. They are full of character, which is no doubt fashioned by the environment in which they survive. Better communications (not least the high-speed train that crosses from Madrid to Sevilla) are slowly bringing improved prosperity, and the new wines of the *Meseta* are unrecognizable from those that went before.

THE MESETA

In this part of the world a *Meseta* is a Castillian plateau or tableland, but more than that the word is essentially associated with the great central plain of Spain that covers most of Castilla-León and Castilla La Mancha, north and south of Madrid.

THE DO LA MANCHA

This is the largest demarcated wine zone in the world, covering some 180,000 of the 600,000 hectares of vineyards on the *Meseta*. Ninety per cent of the vineyards were planted with white Airén vines, producing wines that were dismissed as being acceptable only in the poorest bars of nearby cities, or for distillation.

Led by a progressive Regulating Council, the region is stepping up its pursuit of better-quality and new-wave wines, and although Airén still dominates there is a concerted drive to introduce more red vines, not least Tempranillo. Certainly they seem to be fufilling the prophesies of the likes of Robert Parker and Robert Joseph, who both stated that everyone else should look out once La Mancha gets its act together. Well, it is, so the competition had better watch out.

Almansa

Like Yecla before it, Almansa is a region where one company is the sole disciple for the wines. Bodegas Piqueras have been making first-class reds for several years, but no one has seen fit to follow in their footsteps, although not so far away at Bonillo, and outside the DO, Manuel Manzaneque is making very good Syrah and Tempranillo with Cabernet Sauvignon.

Airén

Airén is the single most widely planted vine in the world, yet it is planted only in Spain and 99 per cent of it in only one region, namely Castilla La Mancha. The rest of the world must have known something. There can be no better example of a vine chosen for its adaptability to a region's conditions, rather than the characteristics of its fruit. Growing low to the ground, its large leaves act as parasols to the grapes and trap the evening dew throughout the searingly hot summer. Unfortunately though, the wines are unremarkable and we can expect a lot of the vines to be replaced.

Valdepeñas

In the far south of the *Meseta*, Valdepeñas has established a reputation for good, soft, oak-aged red wines made with Tempranillo. Meaning 'Valley of the Stones', the sandy clay and chalk soil vineyards are littered with stones that retain the heat at night and improve water retention. Valdepeñas is a small town devoted to wine, though many Bodegas in the white-walled streets have closed down. The competition is intense and they have been unable to compete with the more enlightened companies.

On the main road south you can't miss the huge, hi-tech winery of Felix Solis and Viña Albali, on the bypass, but will probably hardly notice that of Los Llanos, next door. The latter company has buried its enormous ageing cellar underground. Business for Valdepeñas wines was formerly based on the bar trade of Madrid, to which trainloads were sent every week, but the Costa del Sol, with its millions of tourists, has become an equally important destination over recent years.

In the mountains to the west are mercury mines and the castles and towns of the knights of Calatrava. If you ever stay at the Parador (an old Franciscan Convent in the charming town of Almagro) on a hot day, your likely wishes will be answered when you open the Prayer Cupboard in your room, for in it you will find a minibar.

CASTILLA

Castilla is a recently registered *Vino de la Tierra* that embraces all of the vineyards outside the five demarcated regions of Castilla La Mancha. Through an initiative of the Autonomous Government, the European Union has agreed to subsidize the replanting of a percentage of the vineyards with a wider selection of vine varieties, some trained on posts and wires supported by drip irrigation. This is a positive move that ensures a better future and more prosperity for the region than the previous intention of asking the vineyard owners to grub up vines and leave the land to fallow. Vines need less water than any other viable commercial crop, and their continued presence under these new conditions is a guarantee that private investment will follow.

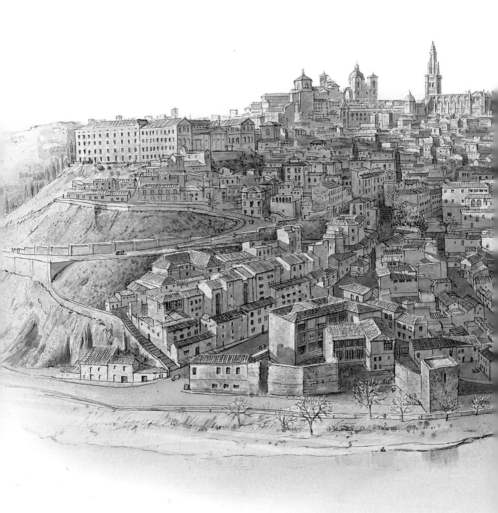

THE MONTES DE TOLEDO

In the north-west of the *Meseta*, near Toledo city, are some exciting wine estates. Most prominent is that of Carlos Falco, the Marqués de Griñon, who is unquestionably one of the pioneers of the Spanish wine revolution. Through his own expertise as an agronomist, and the services of several foreign experts, he has established a reputation for excellence in his wines.

Carlos Falco owns Dominio de Valdepusa at Malpica, where he grows barley, linseed and sunflowers, hunts the local boar and gamebirds, but above all, devotes his time to the twenty or so hectares of vineyards he

started planting back in the 1970s. Falco's first wine was a superb Cabernet Sauvignon blended with a little Merlot, which was later followed with a superb Syrah and a very good Chardonnay. An unusual experiment with Petit Verdot has impressed his Bordeaux advisor immensely, to the extent that he is planting Viognier, a white Rhône variety that he describes as a hot country vine. Under the Marqués de Griñon label he produces Rioja Wines at Ollauri; wines of the Duero valley, called Durius; and an excellent range in Argentina, near Mendoza in the Andean foothills.

Petit Verdot

This is a most unusual grape to find sold as a single variety, because it is invariably blended with other classic French red varieties. The wine is deeply coloured, having spicy and fragrant aromas, with good alcohol and tannins delivering a smooth long finish.

MADRID

What a great name for a wine region, because it is instantly recognizable. However, the wines do not yet match the prestige of the name. Vinos de Madrid, for that is the full name of the region, is divided between the east and west sides of the city with many of the vineyards scattered among urban developments. Mainly planted with Tinto de País and Garnacha red varieties, they appear to be in a pincer of prosperity with, on the one hand, 3,000 restaurants on their doorstep but, on the other, competition for their vineyard land with property speculators. While the vineyards in the Gredos foothills have altitude in their favour, the climatic conditions of the vineyards around Arganda and Chinchón seem to yield better fruit. They are beginning to make some good wines, especially the producers Ricardo Benito and Orusco, who stand out from the rest – oh and keep an eye on Francisco Casas.

OLIVES

The Olive is the fruit of the Mediterranean and Spain grows more than any other country. The serried ranks of trees march across the hills and plains of the southern Meseta, Andalucia and Cataluña, in many places dominating the skyline. It is, of course, a popular appetiser, but olive oil is now seen as the panacea to our cholestorol problem and the increasing demand from cooks all over the world is stimulating better quality through ever-improving production and refining processes.

Extremadura

A rugged, infertile, hot and inhospitable land with diseased old cork trees and stunted vines was the impression I had of the land of the Conquistadors. It was said they all went off to the Americas because there was nothing here, and for years nothing much changed. Well, if you want an example of how improved roads can open up a region, this is it. But before the roads were worked on another change took place: in the 1950s a scheme was conceived of damming the River Guadiana and irrigating over 100,000 hectares of countryside, to create a large fertile plain. Coupled with the arrival of modern farming equipment and technology, this scheme has encouraged landowners to return from the cities and share the increasing prosperity and calmer life-style. For years it was said that the region's only assets were the cork forests and the highly prized, black, acorn-fed pigs from which Bellota, the best *jamón* (dried ham) is produced, but to that one can now add tomatoes, avocados and cherries.

Extremadura has been a neglected environment that will suffer as well as prosper from the changing scene, whether in the captivating cities of Trujillo, Merida and Cáceres or the tranquillity of a sparsely populated countryside.

THE DO RIBERA DE GUADIANA

This DO was formed from the combination of five *Vinos de la Tierra*. The wines are good and the best could be described as decent alternatives to traditional Riojas, at half the price. The very active Consejo Regulador is based in Almandralejo, in the Tierra de Barros, which is the largest and most important part of the zone. The elements of traditional and unsophisticated wine production are still very much in evidence, mainly owing to the inevitable conservatism, but also because of lack of funds.

Brands like Lar de Barros and Monasterio de Tentudia are extremely successful both in and outside Spain. These are the pioneers for others who have to reject sentiment, get rid of the poor vine varieties and start making wines that reflect the real potential of the region. Tempranillo, Garnacha Tinta and Pardina are the three indigenous red and white vine varieties that should stay, along with the inevitable foreign varieties. There is a lot of interest in Sauvignon Blanc and perhaps it will establish a foothold.

PARDINA

Pardina is an underrated, scented white variety with reasonable acidity. Producers need to have more confidence in it, because it yields attractively delicate, floral wines.

JAMON

This is air-dried ham. The legs of pork, around five kilogrammes each, are basted in sea salt and hung to mature for at least 250 days. The most reasonably priced, and most widely available type is the *Serrano*, for which the pig's diet is a mixture of herbs and industrial foodstuffs. But it's well worth taking out a mortgage to try the pricey but tender and sweet *Bellota*, for which the diet is acorns, herbs and mushrooms from the cork forests. The skill of the cutter is crucial, because the ham must be properly and finely cut.

Cava

One of the success stories of the latter years of the twentieth century has been the love affair of consumers with Cava. Still described as Champagne (*Champan* in Spain) by too many people, this is the Spanish sparkling wine that is made by the same method as the French version. That is to say, the second fermentation takes place in the same bottle in which the wine is sold. But although the production process in the Bodega is identical, the raw materials and their environment are very different. The soil, the climate and the grape varieties all differ. Cava is an individual product not to be compared.

In Australia and the United States they call any wine with bubbles 'Champagne', no matter how the bubbles got there. The French have waged a crusade to stop the use of their name on sparkling wines produced elsewhere, but like many old and traditional terms, the change is taking time to take a hold. Much to many people's surprise, the results of this crusade have been to Cava's benefit.

ORIGINS

Cava style wines were first introduced into Spain by José Raventos in the mid-nineteenth century, and by 1900 they were well established with royal approval. The growth of the business in recent years has coincided with the reduction of the length of time the wines were aged. Previously, and in keeping with the traditional Spanish palate, the maturation period before recorking was for longer periods than in Champagne, so the new style Cava wines are lighter and fresher and more appealing.

CAVA CULTURE

Historically Spaniards have treated Cava very formally, which is such a shame when it is an easy and affordable drink. I would love to see a slogan adopted such as *'Toma una copa de Cava cualquiera'* ('Take a glass of Cava whenever you want') because that is how such a cheery wine should be enjoyed. By all means drink Cavas at festivities like weddings and Christmas, but it is also a great aperitif. Personally, I love a glass before dinner, at home or out, and favour any restaurant that offers Cava as an aperitif, especially if it is, or appears to be free.

Consumption of Cava in Spain is not as widespread as one might expect, though it is better than for Sherry. Almost certainly this is a hangover from the more parochial days of difficult communications, so the easier travel conditions, coupled with Cava being produced in more regions across the country, will help remedy the problem. Cava wines are now produced in parts of the autonomies of Aragón, Cataluña, Navarra, La Rioja, Extremadura and the Communidad Valenciana, and all within the realm of the Cava regulations, while a number of sparkling wines made by the same process are being made outside these areas.

GIANTS

By far the largest centre of production is Cataluña, not least Sant Sadurni d'Anoia where the two biggest houses have their installations. The industry is dominated by two groups of companies, namely Codorníu and Freixenet, who battle it out for supremacy, being responsible between them for some 80 per cent of all sales. Cuvee

Raventos, Rondel, Carta Nevada and Cordon Negro are a few of their ubiquitous brands.

BLACK AND BLUE BOTTLES

So intense is the competition, that both Groups have tangled over rights to use certain coloured bottles. As most readers must know, the black one is the trademark of Freixenet's famous Cordon Negro brand, which is one of those magical pieces of branding and marketing that has succeeded beyond even the owners' wildest dreams. Meantime, blue bottles are becoming fashionable; Harvey's Bristol Cream Sherry and Mar de Frades Albariño are two examples, and now a smartly repackaged Rondel Brut for which Codorníu have great hopes.

SMALL AND PRESTIGIOUS

Nevertheless there are a large number of smaller houses benefiting from the increase in interest in Cava and with some first class wines. Although it is invidious to pick examples out of so many, Agusti Torello, Chandon, Juvé y Camps, Cavas Hill, Llopart, Pares Balta, Parxet, Perelada, Rovellats and Vallformosa are a small selection of prestigious producers with reputations for being among the most elite establishments.

PARELLADA

The vast majority of Catalan Cavas are made from Xarel-lo, Parellada, Macabeo and Monastrell grape varieties, with a few using Chardonnay and Pinot Noir, especially for blending. The other regions mostly use Macabeo (Viura). Paradella provides structure and acidity. It ripens late, which is not a problem in the ambient Catalan climate, but still comes in with a surprisingly low potential alcoholic strength.

The Parellada grape variety should not be confused with the famous Cava house of Perelada, whose headquarters are in a village of that name near Figueras in the Dalí country of northern Cataluña.

BARCELONA

All this mention of Cataluña makes me realise that I cannot finish without mentioning the vibrant city of Barcelona. Port, university town and international trading centre, it captivated the world when it staged the Olympics in 1992. The huge success of that event was no surprise to many of us. The practical and businesslike Catalans with their flare for creativity and organisational ability was clearly demonstrated. Of course, they do not reserve those qualities only for such occasions.

Some Other Thoughts ...

Without pretending to cover the ground comprehensively, I am finishing with what I hope are a few tips to help you get the best out of the wines you drink. I feel particularly strongly about the type of glasses that are used, because the wrong glass can destroy the years of efforts of even the best winemakers, and ruin our enjoyment of one of life's great pleasures; good wine with good food.

WHAT TO DRINK WITH WHAT

I started in the wine trade longer ago than I care to remember, when the business in Britain was Dickensian. In those days it was *de rigueur* that meat was accompanied by red wine, and fish by white. However, I was fortunate enough to have an enlightened boss who believed it was best to drink what you like, so if that meant Sauternes with steak, so be it. Of course few would pretend those two make a promising match, and there is a set of rules worth following if you have no difficulty enjoying a wide range of wines.

However, the rules are more flexible than the rule book suggests. For example, Pedro Subijana of the three-star Akelarre restaurant in

San Sebastian demonstrated this at a dinner he prepared at the Dorchester in London. He served a red Rioja with grilled turbot on a bed of red and green grilled peppers. Needless to say, this is just one example of many. So to hell with convention. Drink what you like or feel you will best enjoy at the time.

WINE GLASSES

Key to getting the best enjoyment from a wine, any wine, are the glasses. They should be clear, large and tulip-shaped so that your senses (eyes, nose and palate) can all enjoy the experience. I once heard of someone who put a cube of ice in his glass so that his ears could join in too, but I do not recommend that unless you want to chill or dilute the liquid.

The colour of a wine is a greater part of the enjoyment than is often realized. For example, a bright, pale gold white, or a rich golden brown Sherry, or a brilliant ruby red lend an expectation for what is to come. Clear wine glasses allow your eyes to take in the liveliness the colour suggests. I would also add that a wine with shimmering brilliant colour is inevitably a well-made wine.

Size is important. Wine must have room in which to swill around, showing off its legs and releasing its aromas. Large glasses are not ostentatious, just practical. The tulip shape concentrates the aromas at the opening of the glass, releasing the fruits and flavours to your mouth.

All this is not purist claptrap but rather the way to get the best from a wine. The right glasses allow all three senses to enjoy even the simplest wine. Of course, like choosing a wine to go with food, don't be tied by such rules, just use them whenever you can.

One of the most infuriating habits of many Spanish restaurants is to give you two small glasses, one smaller than the other, with both being too small. One is for wine, the other for water, and then they put the wine in the smallest. Apart from being the most unfriendly treatment of any half-decent wine (or customer for that matter), they must inevitably sell less. Perhaps there is more profit in water.

BREATHING AND DECANTING

There are two schools of thought on how effective it is to pull the cork and leave the bottle to breathe. Some people ridicule the idea because the neck is so small. I say it is better than nothing but probably better still is to pour a small glass and check the wine for any fault at the same time. One can also serve the wine a few minutes before it is to be drunk, so that it can breathe in the glass.

Decanting is a practice originally designed to separate the wine from any lees or deposits in the bottle. However, since wines are being drunk younger, decanting is seldom necessary for Spanish wines, even old ones, because the impurities are removed during the longer period the wines spend in barrels.

Breathing by decanting is not a widely used technique, yet immensely obvious, but perhaps people think it is pretentious. The fact is it is not, it is merely practical. This applies especially when we buy wine in a restaurant, because we drink it straight after the cork has been pulled. I believe we should encourage more decanting in restaurants and at home. Young wines frequently benefit from being 'splashed' over into a carafe, and this can also apply to some *Crianzas*. With *Reservas* and *Gran Reservas* we need to be more respectful, and they should be decanted or poured out more carefully.

CORK AND CORKED WINE

Cork production is exclusive to the Western Mediterranean and Spain is responsible for one quarter of it all. Extremadura in southwest Spain, accounts for half of Spain's share followed by Cataluña, parts of Andalucia, and Toledo. New trees take 29 years to produce the first viable crop, and then only yield new cork every nine years.

The blame for all 'corked' wine cannot be laid at the door of the cork industry, the subject is very complicated, but the incidence of bad cork flavours in wines increased during the last years of the 20th century and even cork producers agree they had become complacent. Without the demand for cork wine closures, the cork industry would not survive, yet many believe the wine industry could manage without cork. This makes the neglect in the farming and processing of cork the more difficult to explain, though strenuous efforts are now being made by Cork producers and the European Union to redress the matter.

Between one in twelve and one in twenty bottles of wine are tainted with the musty taste of bad cork. This is a frightening number, the more so because many people don't know what corked wine tastes like, and even when they do, don't necessarily recognize it. We all have tasting blind spots, conveniently mine is alcohol.

My main concern is that one 'corked' bottle can destroy a person's taste for a particular type or brand of wine, or even all wines in general, especially if they are new to the subject. I believe the solution is to use synthetic or specially manufactured compound corks with all wines (whites more than reds, perhaps) that are meant to be consumed within two years of the vintage. Nowadays this is not the heresy it might seem, because of the sophisticated types of synthetic corks that are available. In fact many prestigious multiple retailers are insisting on such corks before they purchase young wines.

OTHER WINE FAULTS

There are other, more obvious, faults such as vinegar (excess acetic acid), beeriness (oxidization) or a sulphury nose that can be very evident on delicate white wines if drunk soon after bottling. A sulphury nose will often breathe off quite quickly, but if a wine is cloudy you need to take action: despite the fact that this can be the result of a good wine that has been poured badly you should have it replaced nonetheless, because the settlement of any sediment can take ages. Besides, the wine may be 'off'. If you are in a restaurant, ask the staff to replace it immediately; if you bought it from a shop, take it back as soon as possible. No restaurant should ever reject a complaint about wine – complaints are a risk they take, like a tough steak. Besides the profit margins are big enough to cover the odd bad bottle, and most suppliers will replace or refund such bottles if the complaint is made straight away. And, if the customer is wrong, the wine can always be served by the glass or used in the kitchen.

THE DENOMINATIONS OF ORIGIN
FOR WINES IN SPAIN

GALICIA

1 Rias Baixas
2 Ribeiro
3 Ribeira Sacra
4 Monterrei
5 Valdeoras

CASTILLA-LEÓN

6 Beirzo
7 Cigales
8 Toro
9 Rueda
10 Ribera del Duero

PAÍS VASCO

11 Bizkaiko Txakolina
12 Getariako Txakolina

LA RIOJA

13 DOCa Rioja
Cava

NAVARRA

14 Navarra
DOCa Rioja
Cava

ARAGÓN

15 Campo de Borja
16 Calatayud
17 Cariñena
18 Somontano
Cava

CATALUÑA

19 Costers del Segre
20 Conca de Barberá
21 Pla de Bages
22 Empordá-Costa Brava
23 Alella
24 Penedés
25 Tarragona
26 Priorato
27 Terra Alta
Cava

COMMUNIDAD VALENCIANA

28 Valencia
29 Utiel-Requena
30 Alicante
Cava

MURCIA

31 Yecla
32 Jumilla
33 Bullas

CASTILLA LA MANCHA

34 Almansa
35 Valdepeñas
36 La Mancha
37 Mondéjar
38 Méntrida

COMMUNIDAD DE MADRID

39 Vinos de Madrid

EXTREMADURA

40 Ribera de Guadiano
Cava

ANDALUCIA

41 Condado de Huelva
42 Jerez-Xérès-Sherry
43 Montilla
44 Málaga

ISLAS BALEARES

45 Binissalem

SANTA CRUZ DE TENERIFE - ISLAS CANARIAS

46 La Palma
47 El Hierro
48 Ycoden-Daute-Isora
49 Valle de Orotava
50 Tacoronte-Acentejo
51 Abona
52 Valle de Güímar

LAS PALMAS - ISLAS CANARIAS

53 Monte Lentiscal
54 Lanzarote

ARAGÓN, CATALUÑA, EXTREMADURA LA RIOJA, NAVARRA, COMMUNIDAD VALENCIANA

55 Cava

56 DO Catalunya embracing the other 9 DOs of Cataluña.

Four more DOs are anticipated very shortly:
Gomera in the Canary Islands
Manchuela in Castilla La Mancha
Pla de Llevant in the Balearics
Valdejalón in Aragón

112

BILBAO

11 12

EÓN

BURGOS

13 14

15

7

9 10 16 17

ZARAGOSA

18

19 20 21 23

24 25 26

22

BARCELONA

27

NCA MADRID

37

38 39

36

29

VALENCIA

MENORCA

45

MALLORCA

28

34

32 31 30

35 33

30

IBIZA

ALICANTE

A 43

GRANADA

44

MALAGA

ISLAS CANARIAS

LANZAROTE

54

LA PALMA
46

TENERIFE

48.49.50

47

GOMERA 51

EL HIERRO

52 53

GRAN
CANARIA

FUERTE
VENTURA

VINTAGE CHART FROM 1989 TO 1998

These judgements are a combination of my own assessments and those declared by the Consejos Reguladores. Always remember that there are some good wines in not such good years, and a judgement made a year after the vintage can sometimes prove wrong in the long run, since wines quite often mature better than anticipated.

SELECTED DENOMINATIONS OF ORIGIN

	'89	'90	'91	'92	'93	'94	'95	'96	'97	'98
Alella	MB	MB	E	B	E	MB	MB	MB	E	MB
Alicante	B	MB	B	B	B	B	B	B	B	B
Almansa	E	B	B	MB	MB	MB	MB	B	B	MB
Bierzo	MB	MB	MB	MB	D	MB	B	MB	B	MB
Binissalem			B	B	B	E	B	B	MB	MB
Calatayud	MB	B	B	B	MB	MB	B	MB	B	MB
Campo de Borja	MB	B	MB	MB	B	B	B	B	B	MB
Cariñena	B	MB	MB	MB	MB	B	B	MB	R	MB
Cava	B	MB	B	MB	B	MB	B	B	MB	B
Chacoli de Getaria	B	B	B	B	B	B	B	B	B	B
Cigales			B	B	B	B	B	B	B	B
Conca de Bareberá	B	B	B	MB	R	B	MB	MB	B	MB
Costers del Segre	B	B	MB	MB	MB	R	B	B	B	MB
Emporda de Costa Brava	MB	B	MB	B	MB	B	MB	MB	R	B
Jumilla	B	B	MB	B	MB	B	B	MB	MB	MB
La Mancha	B	B	B	MB	E	MB	B	MB	MB	MB
Mentrida	B	B	B	B	B	B	B	B	B	B
Navarra	MB	MB	B	B	MB	MB	E	MB	BMB	
Penedés	B	B	MB	B	MB	B	B	MB	MB	MB
Pla de Bages									MB	MB
Priorato	B	B	B	MB	E	MB	E	MB	B	MB
Rias Baixas	E	E	B	B	B	B	MB	MB	MB	B
Ribeiro	MB	MB	B	B	B	MB	MB	B	MB	B
Ribera del Duero	E	E	MB	B	R	MB	E	E	B	MB
Rioja	MB	E	MB	B	R	E	E	MB	B	MB
Rueda	B	B	B	B	B	B	B	MB	MB	MB
Somontano	MB	MB	MB	MB	E	E	E	MB	B	MB
Tacoronte-Acentejo					B	B	MB	B	MB	MB
Toro	MB	MB	E	B	MB	E	MB	MB	B	MB
Utiel-Requena	R	R	B	MB	E	MB	B	MB	B	MB
Valdeorras	B	B	MB	B	R	MB	B	B	E	B
Valencia	R	R	B	B	MB	MB	B	MB	B	MB
Vinos de Madrid			B	B	B	MB	B	B	B	MB
Yecla	B	B	B	B	B	B	MB	MB	B	MB

E *Excellente/Excellent* MB *Muy Bueno/Very Good* B *Bueno/Good*
R *Regular/Average* D *Defectivo/Defective*

THE MAIN GRAPE VARIETIES

INDIGENOUS
GRAPE VARIETIES

RED

Tempranillo/Tinto Fino/Cencibel
Garnacha (Grenache)
Monastrell (Mourvèdre)
Graciano
Mencía
Cariñena/Mazuelo
Bobal
Listán Negro

WHITE

Albariño
Godello
Verdejo
Xarel-lo/Pansa Blanca
Torrontes and Treixadura
Parellada
Pardilla/Pardino/Albillo
Viura/Macabeo
Palomino/Listán Blanco
Moscatel
Malvasía
Pedro Ximénez
Airén
Merseguera

FOREIGN
GRAPE VARIETIES

RED

Cabernet Sauvignon
Merlot
Syrah
Pinot Noir
Cabernet Franc
Petit Verdot

WHITE

Chardonnay
Sauvignon Blanc
Gewürztraminer
Viognier

LIST OF ILLUSTRATIONS

BIBLIOGRAPHY

Radford, John, *Wines from Spain Education Notes*, Instituto Español de Comercio Exterior

Robinson, Jancis, *Vines, Grapes and Wines*, Mitchell Beazley

Robinson, Jancis (ed.), *The Oxford Companion of Wine*, Oxford University Press

Watson, Jeremy, *Research Reports into the Wine Denominations of Origin in Spain*, ICEX

Williams, Mark, *The Story of Spain*, Santana Books